# Did Jesus go to Church?

## and 51 other Children's Sermons

### Graham R. Hodges

Abingdon

Nashville

DID JESUS GO TO CHURCH?
*AND 51 OTHER CHILDREN'S SERMONS*

## Library of Congress Cataloging in Publication Data

HODGES, GRAHAM R.
  Did Jesus go to church, and 51 other children's sermons.
  Summary: A collection of fifty-two sermons for youngsters
which will help them become closer to God.
  1. Children's sermons. [1. Sermons. 2. Christian life] I. Title.
BV4315.H516        252'.53        81-20585        AACR2

### ISBN 0-687-10762-8

MANUFACTURED BY THE PARTHENON PRESS AT
NASHVILLE, TENNESSEE, UNITED STATES OF AMERICA

# Contents

# Preface

As in my six previous books of children's talks and sermons published by Abingdon, the fifty-two in this one are intended for use by and for children—the book having as its main purpose the leading of boys and girls closer to God. They are for use in churches and church schools, summer camps of all kinds, public schools, vacation church schools, family devotions, and for reading by children themselves. I suggest a prayer by the leader using these pieces, relating the prayer, of course, to the topic.

Some of the scientific illustrations chosen may seem to some to be over the heads of children, but we must remember that concepts unknown to adults when in grade school are now discussed everyday by our children and grandchildren. Also, is it not proper that the church take the initiative in revealing to children the relationship of God to advanced scientific thought, instead of having him ignored as they may read or hear elsewhere?

Some of these talks were given first as children's sermons in Emmanuel Congregational Church, United Church of Christ, Watertown, New York, where I was pastor for nearly twenty-four years.

With great love and affection, I dedicate this book to our three grandchildren—Caroline Jane, Maison Graham, and Rosemary Lynn.

Graham R. Hodges
Liverpool, New York
January 1982

# From the Bible

## Miriam, Moses' Older Sister

1

*Then his sister said to Pharaoh's daughter, "Shall I go and call you a nurse from the Hebrew women to nurse the child for you?" Exod. 2:7*

One of the Bible's most thrilling stories is how the baby Moses was saved from death by his loving mother and quick-witted older sister Miriam. Let us review it.

Pharaoh, king of Egypt over three thousand years ago, feared that the Hebrews were growing so numerous that they would endanger his kingdom. They lived in Goshen, Egypt's richest province. They were hard workers and thrived. Though a Hebrew man, Joseph, had saved Egypt from starvation many years before, Pharaoh thought only of the present danger.

So he ordered all the midwives, who helped the Hebrew women bear their children, to kill the infant boys. What a terrible thing, but this Pharaoh ruled by fear and cruelty. The midwives disobeyed his command, and the Hebrew mothers did all they could to save their infant sons.

One such loving mother, Jochebed, made an oblong basket, coated it with tar to make it waterproof, put her infant son Moses in it, and hid it in the tall reeds that grew along the banks of the river Nile.

Pharaoh's daughter, the princess of Egypt, and her attendants came down to bathe at the river. The princess saw the basket, opened it, and at once was charmed by this helpless little baby three months old.

Not far away was Miriam, Moses' older sister, watching to see what would be done with him. Hidden in the reeds, perhaps bitten by mosquitoes and flies and afraid of the snakes and crocodiles that inhabited the river, she was nonetheless, faithful to her watching.

When she perceived that the princess took pity on her baby brother, she came out from her hiding place and, though perhaps filled with fear, volunteered to find a Hebrew mother who would nurse and take care of the baby. She went and got her mother—Jochebed, who took the baby home and cared for him until he was old enough to stay in the palace.

We want to make a couple of comments about this older sister Miriam, one of the Bible's great heroines. First, frightened though she may have been at her watching post, her love for Moses was stronger and overcame any fear. Have you ever been afraid but knew you must do something, regardless, because, in your heart, you knew it was right? Miriam may have known fear, just as you did, but her love and sense of duty gave her courage.

Also, she used her head. God gives us a mind to use for him and other people. Now most of us might not be as nimble-witted as Miriam when she instantly thought of her mother as Moses' nurse, but, even if we think slowly, God wants us to think. That is the way we solve problems. Surely God wanted Moses to live for his great work, but it may have been Miriam's quick thinking that saved Moses' life. Jesus told us we should love God with our mind, as well as with our heart, soul, and, strength.

And, Miriam was loyal. She was loyal to her mother and to her job of faithfully watching over her brother. Even if she had gone to play just fifteen minutes—if the princess had come then, what a different story it could have been.

We all have times when we want to quit something we know is important. We get tired, afraid, bored, or want to do something else. But if Miriam could watch in the reeds, we also can keep to our task until it is finished.

Miriam, Moses' older sister, has a lot to teach us.

## Joseph, the Forgiving Brother  2

*"And now do not be distressed, or angry with yourselves, because you sold me here. . . ." Then he fell upon his brother Benjamin's neck and wept; and Benjamin wept upon his neck. And he kissed all his brothers and wept upon them; and after that his brothers talked with him. Gen. 45:5a, 14-15*

How would you feel if you had ten older brothers who first dropped you into a deep, dark pit and left you to die, then feeling guilty about it, pulled you out and sold you to some travelers going by, to be taken by these strangers to a land hundreds of miles away and sold as a slave? After this crime, your ten brothers would kill a goat, dip your coat in its blood, and take it to your father, who would think some wild beast had eaten you. How would you feel toward them?

The answer is yours to give, but we must admit that it might be hard to feel forgiveness, even for the most charitable of us.

But in a true story found in Genesis, the Bible's first book, the young brother did forgive. For it is the story of Joseph—one of the Bible's longest life stories and very interesting indeed.

Next to Benjamin, Joseph was the youngest of twelve brothers. Jacob, their father, loved Joseph the most, because Joseph was the son of his old age. Jacob made Joseph a long robe with sleeves. When Joseph's brothers saw that their father loved him more than them, they hated him.

Joseph told his brothers how he dreamed that in the field, sheaves of wheat, which represented their family, all bowed down to his sheaf. In another dream he told them, the sun and moon and eleven stars bowed down before him. This made his brothers jealous and even irritated his father, but Jacob kept the saying in mind.

Even so, it was a cruel thing for his ten brothers to sell him as a slave to the Midianites who were passing through Israel to Egypt. But through various circumstances and his own abilities, Joseph rose to become actually the most powerful and important person in that land next to the king, called the Pharaoh. Pharaoh gave him complete power over the stored food that Joseph had advised him years before to save for the upcoming famine. Now, when Joseph's family faced starvation, there was only one man in the world who could save them—their brother and son, whom they assumed powerless or dead long ago.

Many years had passed, and Joseph had changed so much his brothers did not recognize him. When he did reveal his identity he was a forgiving, tolerant, and wise man; instead of punishing them in revenge, he forgave them in love.

The touching scene in Genesis in which the family is reunited and Joseph forgives his brothers is one of the Bible's greatest portrayals of God's love and forgiveness as seen in people. You must read it for yourself.

Jealousy, bitterness, hatred, violence, betrayal— all these are a part of Joseph's story. But love and forgiveness conquered them all, as can still happen today.

It can be that way in our lives, no matter how cruelly people treat us. Jesus told us this, and he lived it out in his own life, praying for those who were killing him as he suffered on the cross, "Father, forgive them; for they know not what they do."

# 3 Learning to Say No

*But Daniel resolved that he would not defile himself with the king's rich food, or with the wine which he drank. Dan. 1:8a*

Over two thousand years ago in Babylon, a famous and powerful king, named Nebuchadnezzar, picked out some young men for training to serve in his court. Naturally, he had selected those who were very smart, with great promise.

Among them were four youths who had been taken captive from their native Israel, hundreds of miles away. They were Jewish, like Jesus was, and their religion had many rules about what kind of food they coud eat. In addition, these young men were sensible about what they drank.

Now the king commanded his cooks to provide all the young men, including the four Jewish boys, with the finest foods and drink available—the best cuts of meat and lots of them, the best wines and all they wanted. The four young men quickly saw that what the king, in his honest intentions, wanted them to eat and drink was not only against their religion but bad for their health.

Their names were Daniel, Shadrach, Meshach, and Abednego. What would they do? They dared not disobey outright. The king was all powerful and quickly punished those who disobeyed him, often with death.

They did this—they asked the steward to put

them on a diet of vegetables and water for ten days to see if they looked as good as the youths eating the rich food at the end of that time, which they did. The steward then allowed them to continue this diet.

Boys and girls today still face the same kind of pressures these four young men faced. Instead of the temptations being too-rich food and drink, they may come in the form of liquor, drugs, and cigarettes. But you do not have to use these harmful substances that may damage your body and brain for life. You can say no, and your saying it may help some friend say it.

One way to say no is to associate with friends who think like you do. They need your support, and you need theirs. Having three friends of like mind probably helped these four young men of Bible times long ago.

You can pray to God for help—to give you power to resist temptation.

Were these four young men lonely? Perhaps, but they had each other, and they had God. That was enough.

Daniel, Shadrach, Meshach, and Abednego. Remember these four names when you need to say no.

# The Little Slave Girl Who Forgave a General

**4**

---

*Now the Syrians on one of their raids had carried off a little maid from the land of Israel, and she waited on Naaman's wife. She said to her mistress, "Would that my lord were with the prophet who is in Samaria! He would cure him of his leprosy." 2 Kings 5:2-3*

---

One of the Bible's finest stories involves a young heroine whose name we do not know, for the Bible does not give it. The story in the Second Book of Kings goes like this.

Israel and Syria, neighboring countries, were constantly at war with each other. In these wars, each would take captive citizens of the other side, bring them home, and use them as slaves on farms, in mines and homes, or wherever needed. It was usually a terrible life but preferable to being killed, depending on how they were treated.

On one such raid the Syrians made on Israel, a little girl was captured and placed as a servant to the wife of Naaman, a mighty Syrian general second-in-command only to the king of Syria.

But like other human beings, Naaman could and did get sick. With leprosy—the most dreaded of all diseases.

Not only does leprosy make one's skin turn as white as paper, but it also makes the victim look like a character on a TV horror show. Slowly but surely, leprosy eats away the ears, nose, eyebrows, and the tips of the fingers and toes. Eventually the victim dies, but not before long months and perhaps years of suffering.

In Bible lands of Naaman's time, to prevent the infection of others, the victims of leprosy could not touch anybody else, not even their own family, nor come closer than six feet to anybody. They had to shout, "Unclean! Unclean!" when others approached. Lepers could not get jobs, use the public wells, or attend church. The life Naaman faced was to join other lepers in roaming the countryside, begging for food. Quite a comedown.

And then came an unexpected source of help. The little slave girl from Israel.

Hearing of her master's illness, the little girl told Naaman's wife about a man in Israel who could cure him. Ready to try anything, Naaman set out, loaded with sackfuls of gold and other precious gifts from the Syrian king for the Israelite king. How he was healed we tell you in another story, but now let us talk about the little slave girl. What was she like?

First, she must have been forgiving. She was a slave yet willing to offer aid to the man who owned her, an enemy of her beloved Israel, the man who perhaps had killed her own mother and father. Instead of being happy at Naaman's misery, she helped rescue him from living death.

She was imaginative. She used her head; she connected Naaman's sickness with the famous healer in Israel. One reason God gives us our memory and imagination is to help others.

She was brave. Though just a little slave girl in an enemy nation, she summoned up enough courage to approach her mistress.

She was kind. Despite any cruel treatment shown

to her, she could not keep quiet when she saw suffering. She offered help. She obeyed the Golden Rule.

What was her name? Nobody knows, but we can all learn a lot from this little slave girl.

##  5    *Naaman, Too Proud to Do the Little Things*

---

*So he turned and went away in a rage. But his servants came near and said to him, "My father, if the prophet had commanded you to do some great thing, would you not have done it? How much rather, then, when he says to you, 'Wash, and be clean'?" 2 Kings 5:12c-13*

---

About seven hundred years before Jesus lived, or about twenty-seven hundred years ago, there lived a mighty warrior named Naaman, who was a general of Syria and second only to the Syrian king. The Bible describes him as "a mighty man of valor." Syria was the main enemy country of Israel.

But the Bible, in describing Naaman, adds this: "but he was a leper." What tragedy in those few words—for a leper was a person with the most dreaded of all diseases. No words can describe the fear of somebody with leprosy. To have it was a living death. We told you more about it in the story about the little slave girl.

So, no matter how brave he was, how many decorations and medals for bravery he might wear on his chest, or how many honors the king had given him, Naaman's future was naught. Within a few months or years, after much suffering, Naaman was going to die of this dreadful disease.

Then the good news from the little slave girl. Naaman went to his king and got permission to seek out this great healer in Israel. The king approved the journey and loaded down Naaman's horses with costly gifts for Israel's king and the healer—gold, silver, and expensive cloth. When Naaman appeared before the Israelite king, the king thought this was a plot to start a war. But he sent Naaman to Elisha, healer and prophet.

Elisha sent a messenger to tell Naaman to wash himself seven times in the Jordan River and he would be healed. Angry, Naaman rode away. First, this lowly foreign Elisha did not come out of his house to see Naaman. That was insulting enough —but to wash seven times in the Jewish river! What was wrong with Syrian rivers?

But his servants were used to his temper. Quietly they said, Master, if the prophet had told you to do some great thing, would you not have done it? Then why not do as he tells you—wash and be clean.

So, Naaman did as Elisha commanded and immediately was cleansed of the leprosy.

How much like Naaman we are. We want to do or achieve something wonderful or great but are not willing to do the little things that make it possible. We want skills and excellence in athletics, scholarship, hobbies, friendship, music, all sorts of good things but are unwilling to perform the acts, routine, movements, and study that bring us what we desire. Sometimes not just seven times are required, as in Naaman's case, but maybe seven thousand. Recently on television, I heard a professional field goal kicker say that for every time he kicked in a football game he kicked five hundred times in practice. And behind all those "impossible" shots in basketball are hundreds of practice shots. Doing the little things.

So it is in our Christian life. Through constant prayer, frequent Bible study, attendance at church events, and association with other Christians, we achieve with God's help our goals in life. Jesus, even Jesus, had to do these little things daily so that he could do God's will.

Remember Naaman, the general, who was wise enough to do the little things so he could achieve the larger thing.

## 6 Were Women and Girls Important in the Bible?

*So God created man in his own image, in the image of God he created him; male and female he created them. Gen. 1:27*

Were women and girls important in the Bible? Did they matter as much to God as men and boys? Were they honored and respected as much by people of Bible times as were men?

Most of the famous names of the Bible are men's names—men who were kings, warriors, prophets, judges, and other important people. Names like

Moses, David, Joseph, Paul, Saul, Elijah, Solomon, Samson, Daniel, Peter, James, John, Luke, and others come to mind when we think of the Bible. How many women's names from the Bible can we think of? After they have named Mary, Martha, Elizabeth, Eve, Mary Magdalene, Sarah, Rachel, Rebekah, Naomi, Ruth, Esther, some people have to scratch their heads.

In Bible times, as now, the human race was roughly half male and half female. Then why do we not know the names of more women and girls from the Bible?

First of all, most public leaders were men. And because family names and property were handed down through the oldest son in the families, girls' names are not mentioned as often as boys'. Also, some girls' and women's names were not recorded. We wish we knew the name of the woman who bathed Jesus' tired, aching feet, the Samaritan woman who gave him water, the Syrophoenician woman with a sick child, the sick woman healed by Jesus' touch, and the slave girl who helped Naaman. But girls and women were important just the same.

In Jesus' day, women and girls stayed home, did housework, helped in the fields, raised children, and managed the house. But very importantly the mother helped direct the simple family worship service each Friday night to begin their sabbath. You can imagine how impressed the small boy Jesus was as Mary, his mother, helped lead the family in prayers each Friday evening.

Jesus' nation treated women and girls with far

more respect than did other countries. Their rights and privileges were protected more.

Many women in the Bible are remembered for heroism and devotion. Ruth, Miriam, Esther, and Hannah come to mind. And of course, the greatest, Mary, the mother of Jesus.

One great thing the Bible does is to make all persons of equal value in God's sight, regardless of their sex, race, color, nation, or religion. We are all God's children. He loves us all the same.

## 7 The Little Boy Who Gave All He Had

---

*One of his disciples, Andrew, Simon Peter's brother, said to him, "There is a lad here who has five barley loaves and two fish; but what are they among so many?" John 6:8-9*

---

Once when Jesus had gone many miles out into the country—far from towns and cities—several thousand people followed him to hear his great teachings. Also, some came to be healed of their diseases. Still others brought friends and relatives to be healed.

As the afternoon came to a close and the sun dropped lower into the western sky, Jesus, ever concerned about people's welfare, asked one of his disciples to find out if food were available for the crowd to eat. Andrew replied, "There is a lad here who has five barley loaves and two fish; but what are they among so many?" We know the rest of the story—how Jesus took these loaves and fish and fed the thousands of people.

Let us imagine the picture. That morning, knowing her son would be gone for hours and would get hungry, his mother had fixed him a lunch. Then she kissed him good-bye and sent him to hear and see this great man they called Jesus, the Master.

The little loaves were about the size of our hamburger buns, not like our American loaves of bread. So, the lad was not heavily burdened with a big lunch. He had just enough for himself for a long day.

Perhaps the disciples shouted out loud, "Does anybody have any food, so we can divide it?" for Andrew found out about the lad's loaves and fish. Some or all of the following questions might have gone through the boy's mind: Why do they want my food? Will I get any back? If I give mine, will others do the same? Why should I give so that these thoughtless people can eat? I have just enough for myself, so why give? Would my mother want me to give to strangers? Will my five loaves and two fish make a dent in what is needed? Since nobody else is giving theirs, why should I?

We cannot blame this little boy if these questions and others went through his mind. But whatever his thoughts, he gave his lunch to the disciple Andrew. And so, from this lad's generosity came one of the great miracles of Jesus.

We all have talents, gifts, abilities, and possessions which Jesus needs. Should we keep them and use them just for ourselves or give them to the

Master, who can multiply them, so that not only are our own needs met but other people's as well? The answer is up to each of us.

Jesus can take our little and make it much and enrich our lives ever so much at the same time. Countless people through the ages have given their lives to Christ and found that they received much more back than they gave to him.

Give Christ the best you have, and the best will come back to you.

# 8 Were the Wise Men Foolish?

*When they saw the star, they rejoiced exceedingly with great joy; and going into the house they saw the child with Mary his mother, and they fell down and worshiped him. Then, opening their treasures, they offered him gifts, gold and frankincense and myrrh. Matt. 2:10-11*

Often I have wondered how the Wise Men in Jesus' birth story felt when they followed the star to Bethlehem and the stable and saw, not people of wealth and power, but Joseph, a working man, and his young wife, Mary, with their baby Jesus lying in a feeding trough for cattle that had been fixed up for him. The Gospel of Matthew says, "They rejoiced exceedingly with great joy," and I believe they did.

Were they disappointed in the surroundings? "What's this?" they might have asked, "A king born in a stable instead of a castle?" Ordinary shepherds, telling of angels and of beautifully strange music they just heard out in the hills. No, despite all the hardships and dangers of a long trip, how glad they were when they beheld this tiny baby lying in such humble surroundings. This, they knew, was the child. The star told them so.

And so they worshiped the baby Jesus. They were wise men, not judging as some people do. They judged by facts, not by appearances. Had they been less wise they might have gone into a huddle and decided, These people are too poor to use these gifts of gold, frankincense, and myrrh wisely. Let us go quickly. But being wise men, they judged Mary and Joseph by the star overhead and left their precious gifts with them.

No doubt Joseph and Mary used these expensive gifts to defray their expenses to Egypt, to which they fled. The gold kept them alive until Joseph could get work there.

Unlike the Wise Men, we often judge people by how impressive they are—their possessions, clothing, cars, house, in what part of town they live, how much money they have. But not so the Wise Men.

What were the Wise Men's names? We do not know, but the word *wise* truly applies to them. They judged by their own mind and conscience, not by what other people might say.

We all have an inner guide called "conscience," which can make us much wiser if we listen to it. How glad the Wise Men must have been because they gave their gifts to Jesus and his parents. And how glad we are also when we give our lives to Christ.

# Did Jesus Ever Get Discouraged?

*Jesus said to him, "Have I been with you so long, and yet you do not know me, Philip?" John 14:9a*

Did Jesus ever get discouraged? Did he ever feel tired or weary and wonder if he was really getting anywhere in God's great work of bringing salvation to the world? Did he ever have the same tired feeling inside that we all get now and then, and some of us often?

We know that Jesus suffered physically on the cross—when the cruel crown of thorns was pressed on his head, when the sharp nails were driven through his hands and feet, when the spear was thrust into his side. What terrible suffering.

But during his lifetime did he have those same inner feelings that get us all down, so that he could truly understand how we all get weary and discouraged? Even some Christians think that Jesus was so strong spiritually, that God gave him such inner strength, that he never felt as we feel. If this were true, then we could honestly say that Jesus did not suffer as we suffer. But it is not so. He did suffer as we suffer.

More than once in the Gospels we read of his discouragement and disappointment, even with trusted friends like the twelve disciples.

When he healed the ten lepers from their dreadful disease, only one came and thanked him. Well might he ask, "Where are the nine?"

At the Last Supper, Philip made a statement that shows how little of Jesus' message had gotten across; our Master asked wearily, Have I been with you so long, and yet you do not understand me, Philip?

Also at that Last Supper, just before he was arrested, tried, and crucified, Jesus' best friends argued as to who among them was the greatest.

Then there was the strong, brave Peter, who boasted that night that he would never forsake Jesus and yet did just that before the rooster crowed three times at dawn.

As for Judas, Jesus knew he was planning to betray him for thirty silver coins. Judas later repented and hanged himself.

As for the other disciples, they ran when the soldiers came to arrest Jesus.

Even his own family did not understand "I must be in my Father's house."

Discouragement is probably a weak word to describe how Jesus must have felt many times. Heartsick would be a better term. Have you ever been "heartsick"? Then you know how Jesus felt sometimes.

What a friend we have in Jesus, for he knows how we feel when we are down. He understands. He cares. And he will never, never betray, fail, or desert you in your hour of need.

# 10    *Did Jesus Go to Church?*

---

*And he came to Nazareth, where he had been brought up; and he went to the synagogue, as his custom was, on the sabbath day. Luke 4:16a*

---

We go to Sunday school and church to learn about Jesus. Many of our Sunday school lessons are about him, for he started our church. Most of the sermons your pastor preaches are about Jesus. So are many of the hymns we sing. All of the Christmas carols are about his birth, and our Easter songs are about his resurrection.

But did Jesus himself go to church? Yes, and regularly. Not exactly the kind of church we Christians attend. His church was called the Jewish synagogue, for Jesus was Jewish, as were all his family and all his disciples. We should never forget this.

Perhaps near you is a Jewish synagogue. Your pastor might take some children there sometimes. The word *synagogue* simply means "house of prayer" or "place of prayer," a building for prayer and worship much like your own church. And like other buildings in the part of the world where Jesus was raised, the synagogues were made of stone. So it is there even today.

Jesus attended the synagogue on the Jewish sabbath, which begins at sunset Friday and ends at sunset on Saturday. On Friday evening he went with his family to the synagogue, where the men and boys who were twelve and over took turns reading aloud from their scriptures, which are what we call the Old Testament.

Their rabbi, which means "teacher," and who is the equivalent of our pastor, gave a talk. There was no piano or organ in the synagogues, for they had not been invented. People sang pretty much without musical accompaniment, as they used to in our Christian churches many years ago.

As a loving son of his heavenly Father and as a faithful Jew, Jesus went regularly to the synagogue. As a small boy, he attended school at the synagogue during the week, sitting with other boys in a circle learning the Jewish alphabet and ways of reading and writing. There were no girls in the classes. The same language Jesus read and wrote is still used. Jewish scholars today have no difficulty reading the ancient writings of Jesus' synagogue. If your pastor takes you to a synagogue, the rabbi will use the very kind of language Jesus used and even the same kind of scrolls from which Jesus took his turn reading.

Though he was a very special kind of son of God with far greater spiritual strength than we have, Jesus still felt that he must attend his synagogue. He must have felt a need to attend. And that is why we go too.

We need to learn about God's word from the Bible as much as we need food, water, and exercise. From the Bible, the minister, and the teachers, we learn about how God wants us to live. And we never outgrow this need. The church is one of the few places in our land where people of all ages, from tiny babies in the nursery to people ninety years old, attend every Sunday. We never outgrow this need.

Jesus never did. Nor shall we.

## 11 Why Did the Lepers Not Thank Jesus?

*Jesus spoke up, "There were ten men who were healed; where are the other nine? Why is this foreigner the only one who came back to give thanks to God?" Luke 17:17-18, TEV. Also read Luke 17:11-19 for the full story.*

Just imagine, if you can, that you suddenly got the dread disease leprosy, which not only makes your skin the color of white ashes but also makes it rough like a snake's skin and actually eats away your ears, nose, finger tips, and eyebrows, so that you resemble a ghost more than a human being. How terrible. This is what leprosy does to a lot of people in Africa and Asia and what it did to many people in Jesus' land and time.

So afraid were well people of leprosy that those with the disease, no matter who they were, had to isolate themselves from the well people. In their misery they frequently got together and formed bands of lepers, who roamed the countryside. They would scream when well people came into sight, "Unclean! Unclean!" so that the well people would stay a safe distance away. Lepers could not take a job, live with their family, drink from the wells, or go to church or school. They lived on the food thrown to them by generous people.

One day a band of ten such lepers saw Jesus coming. Having heard of his great healing powers, they shouted from a distance, "Jesus! Master! Have pity on us!"

What did he do? He healed them all. But of the ten brought back to health, only one came back to thank Jesus. Only one. "Where are the other nine?" Jesus asked, as well he might. Were they celebrating with friends and family, back to their job, or where? No matter where, the nine did not come back to thank Jesus.

But as each of us looks back over our life can we not remember instances of forgetting to say thank you to people who did something great and wonderful for us, sometimes at real sacrifice to themselves? Parents, teachers in school and church, neighbors, relatives—all these and others have helped us. But did we say thanks? Well, a careful examination of our thank-you record might be somewhat embarassing.

Turning the situation around, have you ever done something for somebody and got little or no thanks? It can be unpleasant, can it not?

Maybe those nine ex-lepers said to themselves, *Someday I'm going to have time to thank Jesus.* But they never did. They never got around to saying thank you.

Several helpful lessons can be learned from Jesus' reaction to failure to express gratitude. First, it did not turn him sour on humanity and cause him to quit helping people. He knew it sometimes happened. Next, this story should make us sensitive to what others do for us and keep us careful to say thanks. Also, it reminds us that expressing gratitude requires only a little bit of time. That is all it would have taken for the nine lepers to express their thanks and that is all it takes for us. But how important. Let us be like the one leper who remembered to say thank you to Jesus.

# Object Lessons

## Why Is Plywood So Strong?

*For the body does not consist of one member but of many. 1 Cor. 12:14*

Why is plywood so strong? So much stronger, in fact, than a regular board of the same thickness cut from the same kind of wood? A simple demonstration will prove what I mean (somewhere in the neighborhood is a man with a woodshop with scraps of lumber).

Take a half-inch thickness piece of any plywood a few inches square or oblong. Lay it between two blocks or bricks with its edges overlapping the blocks. Hit it as hard as you want with a hammer, but it will not break. It may dent but not break. Do the same with a one-inch thickness piece of plywood; not even the strongest man can break it with the hammer.

But a one-inch thickness of regular board. One bang, and it will split in two.

What is the difference? Certainly not in the weight or thickness of the two pieces. They are pretty much the same. But come closer and take a look at the plywood. It is made of several thicknesses, or layers, of wood called veneer, which is just another way of saying thin sheets of wood. These thin sheets are stuck together with very powerful glue under great pressure. Notice that the grain, or direction, of the wood alternates with each overlapping sheet of wood. Each sheet is at a right or wide angle to the one above or below it. You might think that this makes the plywood weaker. On the contrary, it multiplies its strength, as we demonstrated with the hammer.

The great church of Jesus Christ is like plywood. It contains all sorts of people, who act and think differently from each other, sometimes even in opposite ways on very important matters. But instead of leaving the church because they think differently, they are all bound together by the love for Christ and each other. A sort of glue, you might say, as the plywood has its own glue. Their very differences make the church stronger. Why?

Because we can all be wrong about something or partly wrong. Nobody is 100 percent correct all the time. By staying together in Christ's church, we can share our differences in a friendly way, even if our opinions are almost opposite in direction, like the layers of veneer in plywood. By staying together and sharing our thoughts and feelings, we strengthen the church.

It does help, we must admit, when everybody agrees on something, but this is rare on important subjects. And as a great American once said,

"When everybody thinks alike, nobody thinks very much."

God gave us minds to think with. Jesus told us we should love God with our minds, as well as with our heart, soul, and strength.

If you happen to think differently from someone else, do not be afraid to express your opinion in a very polite way, but also let them do the same. In that way both learn.

The great Christian leader Paul, in the Bible, the twelfth chapter of First Corinthians, tells us how important are different abilities to the church.

God's church is strong, because it is his; but in our differences, we each make valuable contributions. That is, if we stick together. Like the plywood.

## Using the Bits and Pieces  13

*Many rich people put in large sums. And a poor widow came, and put in two copper coins, which make a penny. Mark 12:41b-42*

Most men who work a lot with tools, making and fixing things, often have small pieces of materials left over from this job and that. They are too valuable to throw away but too small to be sold or taken back to the store for a refund. These men know from long experience that this piece of plywood, this two-by-four, these few feet of wire, or that piece of pipe will come in handy for some unexpected job someday. So, they save these little pieces. We call them scraps, odds and ends (from someone's sewing basket or a nearby workshop, all kinds of interesting material can be found).

Women who sew do the same thing. Instead of throwing away left over scraps of cloth, thread, or yarn, they tuck them away somewhere. They know from experience that at some future time they will come in handy, and it is much cheaper to have them around than to go to the store and buy extra. Many a beautiful quilt has been made from just such scraps.

Making a life for ourselves also consists of using the little pieces, the odds and ends. This is especially true of the odds and ends of time—seconds, minutes, and hours. Yes, the twenty-four hours a day we all have, whether we are rich or poor. How we use the scraps of time has much to do with what kind of people we become, not in the far-off future, but very soon. For example, here is a scrap of forty-five minutes a day, which one has. If used wisely, one could do a lot of things in a constructive way, learning skills important to us. One boy I knew made the high school basketball team because he practiced free throws an hour a day until he hardly ever missed.

Half an hour of Bible reading daily can acquaint anyone with this great book. Just a few minutes of prayer several times daily can deepen our spiritual lives. One great Christian missionary, Dr. Frank Laubach, prayed hundreds of times daily as he went about his work. He used the bits and pieces of time for God.

Thirty minutes a day spent in vigorous exercise

instead of watching television can make your body strong. Any routine repeated each day can add up to your being much closer to some goal important to you. Use your bits and pieces of time.

Jesus was a very busy person. Hundreds of people came to him some days to be healed of sickness. Yet, he always found time or made time to get away from people and, alone, pray to his heavenly Father. He used the bits and pieces of time.

Unlike other gifts, which come to us, time comes to us all at the same rate and speed—a second, a minute, an hour, and a day at a time. Nobody can hoard or store away time. It exists only at this very moment. The past cannot be recalled or put in the bank. The future, even a future as close as tomorrow or tonight, has not yet come. Only this moment is ours for real. How we use these precious moments gliding silently by is ever so important to us.

God wants us to use our bits and pieces of talent, time, abilities, and energy. With his help such use can make us better people, the kind of people we want to be.

## God's Black-and-White Piano Keys  14

*And God saw everything that he had made, and behold, it was very good. Gen. 1:31a*

Anyone who knows much about a piano knows there are eighty-eight keys on a standard keyboard, fifty-two white ones and thirty-six black. The black ones are narrower than the white ones, but if they were as wide the piano keyboard would be so wide that only a giant could stretch his arms to reach both ends. As it is, people with small hands have trouble enough stretching their fingers to cover the various chords.

Why are not all the keys white or black? I never heard any explanation, but comon sense says their being different colors makes them easier to see and play.

One can make music on a piano just playing the white keys, but you can only play one of the many "keys," or arrangements of notes, on the white ones alone—the key of C. Nice, but monotonous after a bit.

If a musician wants to achieve the greatest possible beauty of music on a piano, he or she must learn the other "keys," all of which involve the black keys—B, G, B-flat, C-sharp, D, and the other keys and their many variations of the seven major keys of C, D, E, F, G, A, and B (if the leader cannot illustrate on the nearest piano, some young student would probably be proud to help demonstrate the key of C and the other keys). From these various keys come all the great pieces of music we love. It is all so complicated and wonderful; there is not space here to explain it, even if I could.

This great beautiful world of ours is like a piano keyboard in the unimaginable variety of sounds, sights, colors, people, plants, animals, insects, birds, scenery, and all the other variety of God's creation—just too much to describe here. And the more we know from science about God's great universe, the more we can wonder and be grateful for the variety he has given us. We can only say, "O heavenly Father, how great you are, and we are truly thankful."

God must like variety too, or else his world would not contain such an infinite number of different creations. Though there are 4 billion human beings on earth, anyone of us could easily pick out our parents' or friends' faces from them all. Instead of making life complicated, God's variety only makes it interesting.

Small wonder that the great king David wrote of God's works: "The heavens are telling the glory of God; and the firmament proclaims his handiwork."

Not only does variety make life interesting, but it is also essential, just as the black keys are essential to a piano. Suppose there were only one kind of fish, one kind of bird, one kind of grass, just one vegetable, or one kind of candy? If that one kind suddenly went out of existence, we would have none. Each is important in its own way.

Thank you, God, for making our world so interesting.

## Life Is a Puzzle with a Missing Piece  15

*For our knowledge is always incomplete and our prophecy is always incomplete, and when the complete comes, that is the end of the incomplete. 1 Cor. 13:9-10, Phillips*

In my hand I have a beautiful jigsaw puzzle, one of the prettiest I have ever seen (most homes and church nurseries have incomplete jigsaw puzzles). Only one thing is wrong with it. One of its pieces is missing, a common plight of most old jigsaw puzzles.

Where could it be? Under somebody's living room couch, or under the television set, or maybe dropped inside the lining of the big easy chair. Maybe someday a person cleaning the house will come across it and say, "I've been wondering where it is. Now where is the rest of the puzzle?"

In a way our lives are like jigsaw puzzles with a missing piece. No matter how hard we try or how hard we look, it seems that a part of life very important to us is always missing. Some people seem to have more than one missing piece, due to bad luck, circumstance, or their own wrong decisions.

There are places we would like to visit but cannot, people we would like to meet but have not, skills we wish we had but do not, individuals we would like to have as friends, but something stands in the way, questions we wish were answered but are not, inner hungers we want satisfied but go unsatisfied.

And no matter if we live to be a thousand years old and have millions of dollars and ever so many friends, being human, most of us will have that missing piece with which to contend, something incomplete about our lives.

Now is this any reason for being sad? Not at all, for so many of us have so many blessings we have no reason to complain, though it does seem sometimes that some people have so much, and some so little. But if we accept the fact that in this life a part of it will seem vacant, that itself will help.

Remember the old story about the poor fisherman's wife who got what she wanted, but each time she did she wanted more? She was never satisfied.

The great apostle Paul in the Bible, who endured incredible hardships for Christ, wrote about himself: "I have learned to be content, whatever the circumstances may be. I know now how to live when things are difficult and I know how to live when things are prosperous." Paul learned this secret of contentment by having the friendship of Christ, which makes up for all other things we want but do not have.

No, there is nothing wrong with striving to make our lives as complete as possible, but it does no good to be miserable inside about things we cannot have.

One great unfulfilled desire I have is to explore the antarctic continent. How I would like to see its vast expanse of ice, its towering peaks, its icebergs breaking off into the ocean, its flocks of penguins. Will I ever see these things? No. So I read all the picture books I can about the antarctic. Not the same, but it will have to do.

## *All Dollar Bills Are Worth the Same*  16

God is no respecter of persons. Acts 10:34, KJV

In my hand I hold two one-dollar bills (no trouble finding new and old dollar bills). The artwork, the picture of George Washington, the pyramid, and eagle with wings outstretched look just the same on both. And just the same as on any other dollar bill. But what a world of difference.

One is brand new, fresh from the bank. I am its first owner after the bank. How fresh and crisp it is. Bright and clean, it is just as new looking as the day it was printed.

But the other. What a mess it is. Dirty, grease spotted, torn, wrinkled a thousand times, with its corner torn off. It may have encountered germs as it was shuffled and passed from one hand to another. And what a sad story it could tell, if only it could speak. It has been spent for food, gasoline, milk, rent, clothing, liquor, library fines, bus tickets, and heaven knows what else. Maybe even robbed from a bank or used as ransom in a kidnapping or to buy drugs. Who knows what kind of legal transactions this dirty old bill has been involved in, not to mention any illegal ones?

Just one look, and you wonder if on its next trip to a bank the teller will put it in a separate pile to be sent to Washington along with other worn-out bills to be shredded and burned.

But as different as these two dollar bills are, they have one thing in common: They are both worth exactly the same—ten dimes, four quarters, or two fifty-cent pieces. No more. No less. Each of them buys the same in the store.

In much the same way, God looks at us. No matter what our appearance, age, health, wealth, character, or whatever, he regards us all as equal.

He loves us all just the same. Jesus came to tell us that.

Some of us are mean, ugly, selfish, unlovable, even to our friends and family. Some are sweet, kind, attractive, unselfish, and lovable to everyone. But to God we are all loved just the same. No matter that some of us seem to love and like certain people more than others. God loves us all equally and sent Jesus Christ to save us all from our sins and tell of God's love.

It took me a long time to accept this idea, because I tended to judge people by appearances and how they acted toward me. But now I know that no human being is so mean that they do not get God's great love as much as I do.

Instead of this being a gloomy thought, it is a thrilling one. For there must be times when I am not so lovable myself. Then I want to know that God loves me just the same, as he does. And that is when we need his love most of all.

Perhaps a lot of us are more like the old, dirty dollar bill than the one fresh from the printing press. The worse we are, the more we need not only God's love but other people's. Jesus Christ came to save us at our worst as well as at our best. He died on the cross to prove God's love for all, not just the good people.

# Will You Choose Ladybugs or Poison?

---

" 'Thus says the Lord: Behold, I set before you the way of life and the way of death.' " Jer. 21:8b

---

In my hands I hold two very different things intended for exactly the same purpose (actual ladybugs can be secured in most parts of the country during the warmer months; insect poison easily available).

One can crawl, fly, eat, reproduce itself, and really looks very cute. It is the ladybug. Why is it called the ladybug, instead of the boybug or manbug? I have not the slightest idea.

The other object is a tiny bottle of powder that I took from a large box of it—a poison for killing insects that eat farmers' crops. Mixed with water, it is sprayed either by a slow-moving tractor sprayer or by a low-flying airplane. This poison is manufactured in one of America's large chemical plants. It does kill the insects that eat certain crops, but it also kills many insects we call friendly and in turn kills songbirds that eat these insects. Applied to a field year after year, it may also poison the entire soil. Birds, as you know, eat lots of bugs and worms, and if this poison kills them there are fewer birds to eat the harmful insect pests.

The ladybug, on the other hand, eats only those insect pests that eat the farmers' crops, such as aphids. Ladybugs can be and are purchased in small cartons from California, and more and more farmers are ordering these tiny little friends and turning them loose on their fields instead of spraying poisons. Turned loose on a field, they go to work quickly to eat the pests. Ladybugs poison nobody, they do not sting or bite people, and they do no harm to insects we call friendly.

Now why should boys and girls be concerned about ladybugs and poisons? Very simple, and very important. Because the world you are growing up in must not be poisoned with chemicals. Right this moment we Americans are spraying our fields, forests, orchards, and waters with all sorts of chemicals, so that this year's crop of this or that will be saved from insects.

Each year literally hundreds of millions of pounds of poisonous sprays and powders go into our environment. Just as bad or worse, we export for profit a lot of the poisons we now forbid in this country. Is this the way God intended for us to treat his earth?

Why do we do it? Partly from ignorance. For many years we thought DDT was wonderful because it killed mosquitoes quickly. Then we learned that it also was killing our national emblem—the bald eagle. We passed laws against its use. As we learn more about other chemicals we are using, perhaps we will ban their use also.

One example of how we are poisoning our land is the falling of "acid rain" on our rivers and lakes. Chemicals from our industrial smokestacks drift hundreds of miles, combine with falling rain and snow, and poison waters many hundreds of miles away. Some lakes in Canada and the United States now contain no fish, frogs, or other life because of this acid rain. Yes, we will somehow correct this process, and the sooner the better. You will read a lot about this poisonous rain and how we must stop it.

Some scientists are saying that, not only fish, but pine trees as well, are being killed by the acid rain, corroding away the waxy surface of the pine needles and leaving them a prey to diseases.

We must all work together and prevent this poisoning of God's world. It will take many years of hard work by people of your generation to correct some of the horrible mistakes already made. It will cost money. There will be arguments over how to do it, but clean up God's world we must.

A few years ago a United States government scientist published a book entitled *The Silent Spring*. She predicted what would happen if we continued using the chemical poisons. Some people thought she was crazy and dangerous. But time has proved her right. For interesting reading, get Rachael Carson's books from your library.

We must do as the Bible says: Choose life, not death. Choose ladybugs, not poisons.

# 18 You Cannot See Yeast Working

*Jesus told them still another parable: "The Kingdom of heaven is like this. A woman takes some yeast and mixes it with a bushel of flour until the whole batch of dough rises." Matt. 13:33, TEV*

Before me I have three objects: some yeast like one buys in the store, a pan of unbaked dough all puffy and white and ready for the oven, and a loaf of bread ready to eat (yeast cake or powder from the food store or risen but unbaked dough will illustrate). These three things represent a famous parable, or story, which Jesus told.

He said his kingdom was like the working of yeast in bread. A woman, like Mary his mother, whom he had seen bake bread many times, takes some yeast and mixes it with flour, water, and salt, covers the dough, and then places it in a slightly warm place for a few hours. Quietly, the tiny yeast bacteria, smaller than the eye can see, multiply. They split in two like crazy, then split in two again, and again, and again.

And as they multiply, they form little bubbles of harmless gas in the dough. These tiny bubbles get bigger and try to force their way to the top, literally millions of them. And when the dough is put into the oven they get bigger, expanding the dough several times into the final shape and size of the finished loaf. When the baked bread comes from the oven, it is ready to eat.

Jesus must have had a good reason for comparing this process with his kingdom, for the making of bread is such a harmless, quiet, everyday kind of thing. Every woman in his town of Nazareth baked bread. These are the very reasons he used this example.

First, he knew that baking bread would be something done long after his life. We still do it two thousand years after he spoke these words.

Next, the Kingdom, he says, will come quietly, in such a way that nobody will hear it. Yet, it works just the same as yeast. It takes its own time and cannot be rushed. No use trying to rush yeast; it works only so fast.

We know that Christ's kingdom comes in people, when people accept him as their Lord and Saviour. This is a quiet thing. And when we continue to follow him day after day, year after year, with our appreciation and understanding of him growing and multiplying like the yeast, there is no big noise—only a single human being growing better all the time. And when this happens to lots of people, it is still quiet but very important and powerful. Lots of things change.

Like the yeast, we have to wait for Christ's kingdom to come. Meanwhile doing what we should for him is like the yeast multiplying. Just one day lived for Christ is good, but repeated many times is, again, like the yeast.

Waiting is part of the kingdom—but waiting with a purpose and meanwhile spending our time learning, training, using our skills for him. Certainly this is true in mastering skills we want. Their repetition, day after day may not be very interesting, but the final result, like a loaf of bread, can be.

Learning is like the making of bread. Especially learning in church, where there is not the excitement of some other places. But God's truths learned in church can change us inside and transform us into the Christians we should be.

Truly, the kingdom of heaven is like the making of bread with yeast, exactly like Jesus said.

# Science and God

## Are Outer Space Creatures Our Enemies?

**19**

*By the word of the Lord the heavens were made, and all their host by the breath of his mouth. Ps. 33:6*

One thing has long puzzled me: In the science fiction books and movies and television involving creatures or people from outer space, why are they usually shown as enemies, ready to kill human beings, drink their blood, use their bodies for some evil purpose? Why is this (no lack of material, unfortunately, in nearby newsstands, children's bedrooms—fantasy science fiction magazines about all sorts of weird creatures out there)?

First, we do not know that intelligent beings such as ourselves actually exist on other planets in our galaxy or in other galaxies. We think they might exist, and many scientists are sure they do.

But whether they do or not, we are already picturing them as ready to cut us down. They are our enemies, not our friends. We must be prepared to shoot first and ask questions later; so our stories about them would tell us.

Is it because we tend to fear the unknown, those things and people we do not know, do not understand, and cannot communicate with? "They" are our "enemies." We are the good guys; they are the bad guys.

But if we read the Bible carefully, our feelings toward many people who might inhabit distant planets would not be like this. For in the Bible we read that God created all the distant stars and planets. The nineteenth psalm tells us, "The heavens are telling the glory of God." They declare his glory, not his hostility or hate.

Ancient peoples of the Bible lands lived in areas where there were few hazy or cloudy nights. They were outdoors a lot at night and could see much more clearly than we can the stars and planets wheeling above. So, there are frequent references to the heavenly bodies in the Bible.

In fact, in the Book of Job we find mention of actual star constellations, or arrangements, the very same ones we can see now, for they have changed little since Job lived. Speaking of God's power to create the universe Job says:

"Who alone stretched out the heavens,
   and trampled the waves of the sea;
who made the Bear and Orion,
   the Pleiades and the chambers of the south;
who does great things beyond understanding,
   and marvelous things without number."

Job 9:8-10

Now if God made all the trillions of stars in the universe and all the probably millions of planets where life might could exist, what right do we have to assume quickly that these other habitable planets are filled with people just waiting to pounce on us? None whatever. But if they are like ourselves, afraid of the unknown and with television shows and science fiction like ours, then maybe we have reasons to worry. Maybe they have been brainwashed into believing the worst, just like us. I hope not.

These distant children of God, for that is what they would be if they exist, are our brothers and sisters of the universe. God is their Father and ours.

Many years ago when people lived in small tribes, they regarded other persons just a few miles away as enemies. They fought and killed each other. That has changed. Now we are learning that the nations of the world, though speaking different languages, must learn to live in peace. We are all God's children, equally loved by him.

It might take a bit of mind stretching to believe that residents of other planets can be friendly. But God's universe is a friendly, not a hostile place. If it is his universe, how could it be otherwise? He is in the farthermost star as well as in our town. People living billions of miles away, if they exist at all, must have feelings like our own.

So, if we ever meet them, let our acquaintance begin with a handshake and a smile, not a blast from a ray gun.

*"So shall my word be that goes forth from my mouth;*
*it shall not return to me empty,*
*but it shall accomplish that which I purpose,*
*and prosper in the thing for which I sent it."*

Isa. 55:11

In front of my house in upstate New York stands a giant maple tree probably a hundred years old. It is more than three feet in diameter and very, very high (use a bough from most any leafy tree during the winter when the leaves are off).

A local science teacher told me that tree has at least a half million leaves on it, maybe a million. When I rake them up in the fall it seems like 2 million.

A million leaves. Just think of it. On just one maple tree. Add all the maple tree leaves together in one city, and you have quite a few truckloads swept up on the streets in October and November.

The science teacher told me something else very interesting about all those leaves. Before they are leaves they are buds, formed in the fall, all wrapped up tightly, each with a special little waterproof cover to protect it from cold and ice, and with the entire baby leaf folded and tucked into the bud, ready to pop open and become a full leaf the next spring. Each fall perhaps a million such buds are formed to become next year's leaves.

But in addition to these buds, I understand, are others which are called dormant, or sleeping buds.

We will call them backup buds, for they literally "backup" or take the place of regular buds when catastrophe strikes the maple tree. A very bad drought, an insect invasion, or some other terrible emergency might come in spring or summer. To defend itself the tree may shed the leaves from the regular buds. When the crisis has passed, the backup buds quickly open and become leaves, saving the tree's life.

As these backup buds save the tree in crisis, so God has mysteriously provided resources and strength when our regular forces run out. Just when we cannot seem to go on, God gives us power to do so. Even Jesus, in the Garden of Gethsemene, discouraged and afraid of the cross, prayed to God, and his heavenly Father provided him the necessary strength to face the terrible agony of those last hours.

When wicked men said of Jesus on the cross, "There, we have taken care of him," how wrong they were. God had other plans. Jesus rose from the dead. Today he has millions of followers all over the world.

When that great American Dr. Martin Luther King, Jr., was killed, many said, "That is the last of him," but today Dr. King is more honored than ever. His ideals live on.

When we fail in our efforts to do the right thing, even after we have done our best, we should not feel defeated for God has ways of making his purpose come true. He has the final say-so in this world's affairs. He has his "backup buds."

If God has found a way to keep that old maple tree in my yard alive in bad years, he will see that our efforts for him will not be in vain.

# 21   God Is in the Biggest and the Smallest Things

---

*"Stop and consider the wondrous works of God." Job 37:14b*

---

What is the biggest thing in the universe? What is the smallest? How do we know they are the biggest and the smallest (for information on the atom consult a good encyclopedia; for help on the space telescope, write Lyndon B. Johnson Space Center, Houston, Texas, 77058 and Corning Glass Company, Canton, New York, 13617)?

Only about five hundred years ago, people believed that the earth was the biggest thing in the universe. But it is not even the largest planet revolving around the sun, and the sun is at least a million times larger than the earth. The sun is by no means a large star, but a medium-size one.

And we know that in our own galaxy, or spinning mass of stars, the sun is only one of about 100 billion. This figure is so large we can hardly comprehend it. And the Milky Way, our own galaxy, is only one of countless millions of such galaxies in God's universe. Ours, a typical one, is so big it takes light about a hundred thousand years to go from one side of the flattened out spinning disk of stars to the other. Our sun, scientists think, is about three-quarters of the way from the galaxy's center to its outer edge. It takes the Milky Way around 200 million years to make one rotation, just to go round once, yet all the stars are going around at speeds to make your head spin.

Yes, there are many hundreds of millions of galaxies like our own and many of different shapes. Scientists believe that a large galaxy is the largest identifiable thing in the universe.

What is the smallest? The smallest is one of the many parts of an individual atom. An atom of oxen, hydrogen, iron, or whatever is so small it would take millions lined up straight to make a line across the head of a pin.

Inside each atom is a nucleus, or center, and around the nucleus, spinning rapidly, are electrons. The atoms of heavy elements like gold, lead, or iron have many electrons in various layers, or orbits, spinning, spinning, spinning around the nucleus and not hitting each other. Light element atoms like hydrogen and helium have very · few electrons. Hydrogen just one. Electrons have almost no weight. They spin so far out from the nucleus that it would be like your tying a string to a pebble and swinging it around your head about twenty-five feet away. In between—nothing. So, an atom is mostly empty space. All the material world around us—typewriters, pencils, paper, ice cream, rock, books, bicycles, you name it—is composed of atoms which are largely empty space.

Now inside the nucleus of the atom are many, many parts—many of them also forever moving, changing, and doing all sorts of things impossible to imagine. Scientists have given them names, and you can read about them in your science book or encyclopedia at school or at home.

These various nuclear parts and the electrons are

the smallest things in the universe. God made them all, as he made the largest and most distant galaxies. And he keeps track of them all.

Sometimes in the 1980s our government will send into space by rocket ship a telescope fourteen feet in diameter, to be stationed 310 miles above the earth's surface, where it will observe the universe for us as it has never been seen before. With it our astronomers will see seven times as far as they can now. Objects now far too faint to be seen will be photographed. This telescope will be fifty times as powerful as any now on earth. It will reveal to us galaxies as they were 14 billion years ago and untold trillions of miles away.

This telescope will revolutionize our ideas about God's majesty and power and greatness. Already his universe is too marvelous for description. This telescope will make it even more vivid. I hope that you will read all you can about this telescope as it is being built for transport into space by the space shuttle ship.

God is in the biggest and the smallest things in the universe, for he made them and all that is in between. How truly great he is.

## 22 *The Cocoon—So-o-o Long to Wait*

*And he went down with them and came to Nazareth, and was obedient to them. Luke 2:51a*

Recently, in getting out of my car one cold March day with the snow two-feet deep by my driveway, I saw something odd looking hanging from a lower branch of a young maple sapling. Coming closer, I saw that it was some kind of insect's cocoon, about two-inches long (if a cocoon itself cannot be found, use the pictured description of an insect's life story in an encyclopedia; using both would be better). That would make it a fairly large insect when it emerged from its winter shelter in the spring, maybe a moth or large butterfly.

As you know, a cocoon is a tough, grey, silky-like, longish oval home of an insect during its third stage of life, the four stages being egg, larva or caterpillar, pupa, and grown insect, the one we see flying and crawling around.

By and large, most insects do most of their eating as a larva. We call them worms then, though they are not true worms. When a larva reaches the proper stage, it stops eating and spins this winter home called a cocoon, in which, as a pupa, it survives the cold weather for some months until the next spring. Most of its life it spends asleep in the cocoon. It cannot migrate south with the birds and has developed this way of surviving the cold months. During these months it is neither a worm nor an insect but a mummy-like thing in between. In the spring its body develops the outlines and then the real shape of wings, then eats its way out of the cocoon, stretches its new wings and flies or crawls away, ready to do whatever its bug heredity tells it to do.

I have often wondered, that, if the pupa could think for itself, around February or March, when it has been hanging in one position for some months, how it might say, "How boring it is. Hanging here day after day, week after week, month after month. Nothing to do but hang in this silly position. All alone. Nobody to talk to. Why, nobody even knows I exist. Oh dear, whatever will become of me? This is Dullsville itself."

And why should it not say something like that? We know that something very important is going on inside that pupa's body. We know that all that dull waiting is not wasted, that God has so arranged the pupa's life that these dreary months are necessary. Though most of its life is spent in waiting, these months are not wasted.

You know, much of Jesus' life is unknown to us. From the time he was questioned in the temple at twelve until he started his ministry, almost twenty years had passed. The Bible tells us nothing about these many years except that he was obedient to his parents. So much must have gone on, yet we know so little. We can only think about what must have been the life of a young man in Nazareth at that time whose father was a carpenter.

Did Jesus get bored? Did he often think of those great three days in Jerusalem when he was twelve, amazing the great wise men with his questions? Did he wish he was back there instead of working away quietly in his father's shop—sawing, hammering, planing, fitting this piece of wood and that, repairing doors and windows, or whatever jobs came into the shop? Did he get tired of waiting for that great work that something inside him told him he would do? Twenty years is a long time to wait.

But it was not just waiting. Important changes

were going on in our Master's life. He was observing, studying, working, thinking, absorbing his father Joseph's wise words and loving ways, and perhaps shaping in his own mind the great teachings, which he spoke in the Sermon on the Mount and in the various parables.

Certainly he was deciding how God's Word should find expression in the world. Should it be through military conquest or by the slower and surer method of changing people's hearts? And he must have been deciding on what kind of people would make the best disciples. Yes, in comparison with his few months of ministry, three years at the most, Jesus' life in Nazareth was much, much longer. But it was not wasted time.

Do you ever feel like a pupa must feel around February first? Waiting, not much changing, not a lot of excitement or sense of importance? Well, don't we all? But when we are boys and girls this sense of boredom seems to take over sometimes. We want to be somebody important or do something important. Not ten years from now, but right now.

But these years of being young are not wasted years. Not only can we enjoy them and be happy despite a lot of things, but we should store up knowledge, strength of body and mind, skills of all sorts, increased wisdom in dealing with people, and gradually be finding out what we want to do in life.

It is not wrong to want to be stronger, wiser, better looking, cleverer, richer, more admired by friends all at once, like a superperson. But these changes probably will not happen that way. They take time. Growing up cannot be rushed all that much.

Remember the waiting months of the pupa. Remember that Jesus worked quietly at home in Nazareth for twenty years or more before he began his ministry—not one word about him in the Bible all those years. Then we can understand why we have to be a bit patient as we grow up.

## 23 | The Seas, God's Air Conditioner for the World

---

*And God said, "Let the waters under the heavens be gathered together into one place, and let the dry land appear." And it was so. God called the dry land Earth, and the waters that were gathered together he called Seas. Gen. 1:9-10a*

---

When we think of the oceans, pictures of bathing beaches, fish, sharks, icebergs, and ships come to mind (world maps or globes, plus pictures of the ocean, will do here). How pleasant and beautiful the ocean is, and what pleasure it gives us in so many ways. Everybody likes to visit the ocean. And most of us like to eat the creatures that live in it—shrimp, fish, oysters, lobsters, crabs, clams.

But the ocean performs a quiet, essential function besides furnishing us with good things to eat, and even if we have never seen it at all. As you may know, there are about twice as many square miles of ocean surface as land surface on the earth, including all the continents and islands. The oceans' average depth is two miles, and their deepest places would submerge Mt. Everest, the world's highest mountain, without a trace. The salt in the oceans would easily cover the entire United States a mile or more, with plenty leftover.

But the function performed by the oceans for us all is to be a "weather conditioner." The oceans make our weather. Winds and rains may sweep across our broad stretches of land, but what they bring from the oceans make up our weather. Tiny, microscopic bits of salt are caught by the winds as they sweep over cresting wave tops of the ocean and carry them high in the sky. Later, when these specks of salt, still high in the air, reach the mainland they become the nucleus of raindrops and snowflakes, which fall to the ground.

Ocean breezes move hot stagnant air; otherwise this air would soon suffocate us. If there were no oceans, the world's climate would be extremely harsh, varying from very hot to very cold, far too extreme for human life.

Oceans store up heat in the summer and release it during the winter, aided by vast, circular currents, which take heat from the tropics and move it northward, such as the Gulf Stream, which flows from Florida to northern Europe. Other ocean currents such as the Humboldt Current on South America's western shores, bring cold waters laden with rich nutrients from arctic and antarctic regions, providing food for fish. You can trace these currents on any world globe or map.

Ocean currents north of the equator generally revolve in vast circles clockwise; those south of the equator, counterclockwise. All of them affect the weather and climate in ways we are just learning about. And deep down in the oceans is a slow-moving drift of cold water from the polar regions to the equator, where it is warmed by the sun and sent back again.

God made just the right amounts of ocean and dry land to provide proper climate for all kinds of plant and animal life, whether whales, pine trees, horses, palms, or whatever.

Ocean scientists are finding out many hitherto unknown facts about how the ocean controls our weather and climate. Each discovery only makes plainer how wonderful is God's plan of creation. They are his oceans, as we are his children. As Psalms 95 says, "The sea is his, for he made it; for his hands formed the dry land."

## 24 God's Ways and the Lotus Seed

*But when the proper time came God sent forth his Son. Gal. 4:4a, Phillips*

Why did Jesus not come sooner? Why did God wait so long to send his Son, who would show us how to live like we should? Could he not have saved the world a lot of suffering, given us his teachings a lot sooner, and made the world better long before he did? Why did Christ wait so long to come?

True, it has been almost two thousand years since he did come, but before that the human race had been around a long time, doing all sorts of dreadful things, needing badly the wonderful teachings and life of our Lord.

These questions about his not coming sooner are not easy to answer. At first it might seem that God was not sensitive to people's suffering, but we know that is not so. He does know, and he does care.

Actually, we may never know why he sent Jesus at the exact time he did, but we can be sure that his timing was deliberate, that there were good reasons for his coming no sooner and no later. The great apostle Paul, who lived at the same time Jesus did, wrote, "when the proper time came God sent forth his Son." In other words, just at the right time.

The ways of the lotus seed remind us of this Bible verse (pictures and illustrations of the lotus in any standard encyclopedia will suffice). The lotus is a beautiful plant which floats on the water. It is the national flower of Egypt. One remarkable trait sets it apart from most other plants. The lotus seed can wait for hundreds of years, even a thousand years, before it sprouts. It may sprout the very next year after it is produced, but if conditions are not right it may wait two, three, five, ten, fifty, a hundred, or a thousand years. When conditions are just right, in other words, at the proper time, it will sprout and become a lotus plant.

God's ways are like that. God does not hurry or

act just because we want him to. He would never do something wrong or too soon or too late just because we prayed hard and tried to change his mind about his schedule. If our prayers could persuade him against his will, he would not be God. So, he does things in his own way and time, and it is our task to find out what these are, instead of trying to make him do things the way and time we want.

It takes just so much time to bake a cake properly. We cannot hurry it by turning up the oven. It would ruin.

Some people say that God created the earth like it is in the flash of a second, complete with all the fossils, fish, seas, apes, and people. Let them believe it if they wish. But to me God did a far more wonderful thing in patiently directing through countless centuries the unfolding of our world as it is. He did it in the proper way and time.

Sometimes in our own lives, we want to hurry things too much, especially when we are young. There is not much way for a fourth grade boy suddenly to become overnight a star quarterback on the local high school football team. But in the proper time, with lots of practice and physical exercise, he might make a position on the team. If it were all done by hard wishing, wanting, and praying, then everybody might be a quarterback.

A girl wanting to be a teacher or nurse may have to study and wait for many years, going to high school and beyond, before it can all happen. When the proper time comes, if she has prepared herself properly, then her wishes come true.

God sent Christ at the right time, the proper time. In our own lives, tedious, long waits are sometimes necessary before something we want badly can happen. And while we are waiting, let us prepare ourselves so that it can happen.

## *Has God Finished Our World?* 25

---

*"You, therefore, must be perfect, as your heavenly Father is perfect." Matt. 5:48*

---

Has God finished creating his world, our world? Has he done all that he intends to do with it—changing and rearranging the seas, mountains, plains, rivers, lakes, forests, and fields? Has he said to himself, *There, I am through*?

No, not really, judging by what we can see going on. People long ago believed that God was all through with our world, like an automobile manufacturer is through with a car when it rolls off the assembly line. The world was the same as it always had been, they believed, and always would be, forever and forever.

But no, God is constantly changing it around. He has been doing this since the earth was formed, and there is no sign that he is letting up.

A 100 million years ago, the great dinosaurs roamed the earth, including what we now call the United States (use pictorial material in encyclopedias, illustrated science books, etc.). Scientists find their bones all the time. Mammals had not come on the scene. Only about ten thousand years ago, the giant woolly mammoth and saber-toothed tiger roamed our country.

And more than once have sheets of ice more than a mile in thickness covered most of Canada and the northern part of the United States. The last ice age went as far south as Pennsylvania and Wisconsin, ending only about ten thousand years ago. It left behind thousands of glacial lakes, large and small. The entire land where the ice rested was depressed many feet by the glacier's weight and is now slowly rising again, as a mattress rises when we get out of bed in the morning.

The oceans have crept inland many times, covering parts of the continents. Eons ago an arm of the Atlantic Ocean extended from the Hudson Bay to the Gulf of Mexico, splitting North America. Even parts of the Rocky Mountains were covered.

As for volcanoes and earthquakes, they too have continued through the eons, as our own Mount St. Helens in Washington State illustrates. Their activity reminds us that God is still creating his world, moving things around. Really, the earth is never the same two days in a row, or two years in a row.

The same goes for the larger universe, our solar system, the Milky Way galaxy, and all the other millions of galaxies. Constant motion and change. That is their way. God is still working on them.

Furthermore, God is working with us to help us change too. Helping us to become more loving, forgiving, helpful, and more like Christ. That is, if we want him to. For unlike the physical universe, people can resist change of heart. God does not control us like he does the earth and stars.

Changes of our hearts and minds are possible with God's help. Jesus used the word *become* because it describes possibilities for change. The words in the Lord's Prayer "forgive us our debts" and "lead us not into temptation" are requests to God to help us change for the better.

So, as God is constantly changing his universe, he is willing to help us change also. If we are wise, we will accept his assistance and be the people he wants us to be.

## *Where Is Here? When Is Now?*  26

"*Heaven and earth will pass away, but my words will not pass away.*" Mark 13:31

Where is here? When is now? Will not yesterday be nice? Was not tomorrow a beautiful day? Which way is up or down?

Crazy questions? Of course, but not as crazy as they used to be. For in this universe of ours, this universe of constant change and new discoveries, we are finding out that in the matters of time and space crazy things make sense.

A simple illustration. When we observe a fast plane overhead, we note that the noise from its engines seems to come from somewhere to the rear of the plane, where it was a second or so ago. This is because it takes the sound from the engines just that long to get to us, and by the time the sound strikes our eardrums the plane has moved quite a distance. Sound travels a mile in about five seconds, and if the plane is very high it may have traveled a full mile before we hear the sound it made about five seconds before. In other words, we see the plane in one place and hear it in another.

The same principle applies on a larger and faster scale to the distant galaxies we observe in our most powerful telescopes (modern picture books on astronomy have plenty of good photographs of distant galaxies; consult the local public or school library). The galaxies we see were in the place where we see them several billions of years ago. Even traveling at 186,282 miles per second, it takes the light from a galaxy a long time to reach us from where the galaxy was when the light started on its way to us. It is the same kind of thing we experience with the airplane's sound, only on a far larger scale. Astronomers are seeing these galaxies now as they looked eons ago. They appear in our telescopes as they actually existed billions of years ago, as the plane flying high overhead appears to be far ahead of the place from which its sound comes. The universe as we see it in our telescopes no longer exists as we see it; its appearance and location changed long ago.

So, way out in space there is no up or down, no north, east, south or west. Up and down applies to earth, not to space.

In our lives we also move and live in a fast changing world. As we move to new neighborhoods or towns and cities, we may move among people who have different ideas of what is right and wrong. We get mixed up, bewildered, and confused. But God has certain laws of human conduct that never change with location or time. The Bible contains these laws: the Ten Commandments, the life and teachings of Jesus, the great teachings of the prophets, and many other sources in the Bible that keep our sense of moral direction always true. Though the Bible was written many centuries ago, it contains truths that apply to any time or place.

Jesus' teachings on love, forgiveness, charity, peace, generosity, and sacrifice have not changed. They are valid always and everywhere. And the more unfamiliar our place of living, the more we need to rely on them. He spoke words that apply here, "Heaven and earth will pass away, but my words will not pass away."

His way, his salvation, his truth—the same, yesterday, today, and forever. How glad and grateful we can be for these guidelines of living that never change, no matter where we may go.

## *God and the Trilobites*  27

*Before the mountains were brought forth, or ever thou hadst formed the earth and the world, from everlasting to everlasting thou art God. Ps. 90:2*

Very near to where I live, the Black River tumbles downward on its rush from the Adirondack Mountains to Lake Ontario. As it goes through our area, it flows over rock called limestone (the geology section of any good picture encyclopedia will help here; rock collectors, school science teachers, or mineral-rock shops also). In one place in our city, it has cut a long canyon fifty-feet deep, with roaring waterfalls audible for more than a mile during the spring runoff when the winter snows melt. It roars, hisses, grumbles, and thunders like any other large rushing river.

During the summer dry months it retreats into a much smaller stream, leaving wide shelves of limestone bare and dry. Then I can walk out over this gray rock. Underneath are over nine hundred feet of solid limestone, created over many millions of years of time when a shallow arm of the sea extended far inward into what is now the United States.

Tiny sea creatures of all kinds, most now extinct, lived and died during those eons of time, their skeletons settling on the bottom of the sea, piling on top of each other as the centuries passed, first forming a soft ooze, and then as they deepened, composing a hard stone. None of them weighed much by themselves, but as their billions and billions of tiny skeletons piled atop each other they formed this solid nine hundred feet of limestone that underlies that part of New York State.

Looking at these tiny fossils under a magifying glass, we see that they generally range in size from that of a pea down to a pin head. The largest is the trilobite fossil, easily seen as one walks over the limestone rock. Its name comes from its having three parts.

When these trilobites lived, salty ocean waves rolled over that spot near my home, with sharks and all kinds of now-extinct creatures swimming about.

The lowly trilobite crawled over the ocean floor.

The same beautiful red, gold, green, yellow, and purple sunsets that we now see glowed over that spot when it was part of that ancient arm of the ocean over what is now New York State. That has not changed.

Does this vast change in this spot make me sad or lonely? No, it gives me comfort, that the same God who created the trilobite and his fellow creatures created me. He ruled the ocean waves then, and so he does today. He has not changed.

Unaware as he was of modern science, the Psalmist possessed the same feeling of awe, wonder, and gratitude we have. In Psalm 90 we read, "Before the mountains were brought forth . . . thou art God."

No doubt very near you are evidences of God's creative power eons ago. And certainly in some nearby museum, school science lab, or picture books on geology, you will see for yourself and feel the same reassurance I get when I walk over the gray limestone of the Black River and gaze down on the trilobites' skeletons. God was here then; he is here today.

## *All Horses Run on One Toe*  28

*I can do all things in him who strengthens me. Phil. 4:13*

The horse, one of the fastest animals in the world, runs on just one toe of each foot (any good picture encyclopedia will probably help here, or books specifically about horses). Even race horses do this. We humans cannot stand on one toe, much less walk or run.

The explanation is simple. Scientists tell us that millions of years ago, when the modern horses' ancestors were no bigger than a poodle dog, they had many enemies larger and fiercer than they, who chased them down and ate them.

To escape from these hungry enemies, the little horses developed great speed. Speed and escape became their defense. Then, as now, they ate grass, not flesh. In developing their lifesaving speed they began to run on their toes, as we do when we run our fastest. They ran on five toes, then four, three, and finally, one great big toe, which has developed in size and strength over the centuries. The other four toes receded into the leg structure. They are there today but are not used for locomotion. God helped these animals adapt in marvelous ways to the daily challenge of survival, mainly by the overdevelopment of a single big toe that gave them speed.

Other animals in the horse's dangerous position also developed different arrangements of their five toes. The cow, deer, camel, and some other grass-eating animals use only two toes.

In science studies we learn how God provides many creatures with special adaptations of body so they can survive. Owls' eyes can see at night so they can catch the rodents that roam then. Mosquitoes can stay frozen nine months in the cold arctic and emerge in good health, ready for action. Hummingbirds' beaks are long and sharp for sucking nectar from flowers. Hundreds of other such examples could be listed.

God has given to human beings, not only special physical features for survival, but also qualities of the mind and spirit that conquer adversity. President Franklin D. Roosevelt, crippled by polio as a young man, developed enormous will power, patience, and courage that made him a great President.

Blind people not only learn to move around physically but also develop their courage and sense of humor, and find a way to combat the feeling of self-pity that would handicap them even more.

Scientists call such adaptation compensation. To overcome a handicap we compensate or make up for it. A shy person can overcome their shyness by deliberately forcing themselves to talk to others, look them in the eye, or shake hands with them first. Those of us who procrastinate, or put things off, can adopt the motto "do it now" and get rid of that guilty feeling that goes with the handicap of procrastination. The handicap of selfishness may be conquered by forcing ourselves to think of others first, by praying for others, by seeking ways to make them happy.

The sins of rudeness, greed, timidity, hate, anger, and fear may be overcome by the daily practice of courtesy, courage, love, generosity, and kindness. The apostle Paul had some serious handicaps, but out of his struggle to overcome them he wrote, "I can do all things in him who strengthens me." God will help us, as he helped

Paul. He can take our weak points and make them our strong points. Compensation not only works, it can be fun.

## 29 God's Light and the Prism

---

*"Let your light so shine before men, that they may see your good works and give glory to your Father who is in heaven." Matt. 5:16*

---

A glass prism is nice looking in its own way; really it is merely a piece of finely polished glass with smooth, parallel sides cut in many shapes (prisms may be borrowed from someone's chandelier, from the local school science lab, from most any place). Prisms are frequently used in chandeliers. Some prisms almost look like a huge jewel.

But without sunlight streaming through it, a prism really does not come alive. What a difference the sunlight makes.

Hold a prism up in bright sunlight and then watch the rainbow colors that fall on any surface the light touches. Revolve the prism slowly, and the rainbow colors change.

As the light passes through the glass, it is divided by some mysterious process into lovely bands of color—red, orange, yellow, green, blue, and violet—the same colors you see in a rainbow. Just how, I do not know, but a physicist could tell you, or you could read about it in your school encyclopedia. If you slowly twist the prism in sunlight, the colors appear at the prism's edge also.

How like prisms people are. If we allow God's love to shine through us by doing his will, obeying his laws, following his Son Jesus Christ, doing the things each day we should as his children, then that light which we call love will shine through our lives in dozens of ways, making the world a better place in which to live and ourselves more attractive people. As the prism's colors falling on the nearest surface make the prism itself more attractive, so God's love shining through us influences, not only people nearest and dearest to us, but somehow turns us into people more attractive than we had been before.

A prism kept in a drawer or on the shelf is just another pretty piece of glass. A prism hanging in the sunlight makes its environment as well as itself different. So, if we will not let God's love shine through us we fail in making where we are and what we are better. The prism has not control over itself and where it will be. We do.

And as we allow God's way to be ours, to that extent the world around us and we ourselves are changed by his unfailing love.

## *Seeing Inside the Geode* 30

*"The kingdom of God is in the midst of you."* Luke 17:21b

No doubt you have seen a geode (pronounced jee-ode) or part of one, even though you may not have known its name (sliced geode sections may be found in rock hobbyists' homes, in rock and mineral or gift shops, and probably in a nearby school science lab). According to Webster's dictionary, a geode is "a nodule of stone having a cavity lined with crystals or mineral matter." Geodes, which can be bought in mineral or gift stores or stores where rock hobbyists buy their specimans, look on the outside like a brownish coconut without the fibers, roughly shaped like a ball, very heavy for their size, and running from about an inch to many inches in diameter. Rust color might also describe their appearance.

When sawed through with a sharp, small-toothed power saw, in half or in sections, one can see the most beautiful mineral crystals of various colors. The colors, never exactly the same in arrangement, are determined by the kinds of minerals in the waters that flowed into the geode over many thousands of years.

Geodes originally were little cavities, or hollow places, underground in rock, sometimes very deep underground. As rain waters seeped through the rocks above the geode, they carried tiny amounts of the various mineral deposits lying above. When these waters came into the geode, they left these minerals in the form of crystals that gradually built up, sometimes filling the little cavity, or hollow place. It looked like a fairy had designed and built up the crystals—blue, pink, red, green, and all combinations of colors. And no two alike.

As the rocks above the geode eroded away

through the centuries, the geode naturally appeared on the surface. In some places they are so thick on the ground that bushels can be picked up in a few square yards. Cut in half and polished, they are popular items in gift shops. Surely there is one in your school science lab or in a friend's home. Perhaps one in yours.

Geodes remind me of people. In outside appearances few of us are beautiful glamour people. And as we get older, even what beauty we have fades. Grey hair, wrinkles, all sorts of changes take place.

But inside, in our minds, our spirits, and hearts, that can be a different story. As we grow older, the qualities most important such as kindness, generosity, love, good will, and forgiveness, which we will call crystals of the spirit, accumulate slowly but surely until our personalities become more and more attractive. Sometimes the process of change goes with suffering and pain.

Have you known older people who seem to have a thousand wrinkles on their face but are so sweet and kind you like to be around them? And perhaps you know boys and girls your own age with terrible physical handicaps whose courageous spirits and character make you forget their handicaps.

This change inside can occur in us all, if we let it. Our personalities do not have to become vacant and uninteresting but can develop like the geodes, becoming more attractive through the years. Geodes have no control over what kind or color of crystals they contain, but we do. With God's help, we can become more and more like what he wants us to be.

# Various Topics

## You and I Are Millionaires  31

*Beloved, I pray that all may go well with you and that you may be in health. 3 John 2b*

You and I are millionaires. Millionaires many times over. And all without working a single day or hour for our wealth.

How? Very simple. But so simple that I frequently forget myself how very rich I am. And when I do forget I feel ashamed, for I inherited all these riches without lifting a finger.

I am a millionaire in so many things that money cannot buy. First, with my own two good eyes I can see God's great, good, beautiful world—its plains, rivers, mountains, oceans, sunrises and sunsets, sports and games, art, woods and streams. I would not take a million dollars each for my eyes. Would you? And yet there are many people who cannot see at all through no fault of their own.

Then my two ears hear perfectly—music, voices,

birds, rain drops on the roof, and people's laughter. Not for a million dollars each would I give up my hearing. Would you? But there are millions of people who cannot hear.

And as for my sense of taste, how I would hate to give that up. Not even for a million dollars would I give up the delight of tasting peppermint, vanilla, chocolate, hamburgers, hot dogs, milk shakes, strawberries, and oysters. Yet, many people have lost their sense of taste.

And as for smell, I would not take a bushelful of money for the ability to smell the odor of cooking food when I am hungry, or the odor of roses, bananas, oranges, perfumes, new mown hay, or potato chips at a picnic. Would you?

As for the sense of touch and the kinesthetic sense, so very valuable in so many ways, who can measure their worth in money? None of us would sell them. We enjoy our good feelings, and our bad feelings protect us from harm and danger. The nerves in our skin protects us from burns as well as from freezing.

Our muscular sense, called kinesthesia, tells us how to stand, walk, run, sit, skate, play ball, and a hundred other things involving any kind of movement. Not for $5 million would I sell it. Yet, I did not earn it or any of the other valuable gifts of my body. God gave them to me. Not until they are taken away from us by illness or accident do we truly appreciate them.

And as for friends and family, who can or would put a monetary price on them? Not I. Not you.

Yes, truly if we have all these gifts and so many others I could mention, we are rich. We are rich in things money cannot buy. Not all the gold and silver in the world equals them in value.

So, if you ever get to feeling sorry for yourself, stop it. God has blessed you beyond calculation.

## By Not Changing Seats She Changed Our Nation

---

*I foresaw the Lord always before my face, for he is on my right hand, that I sould not be moved. Acts 2:25b, KJV*

---

It was a cold, raw, autumn evening in 1955 in Montgomery, Alabama. In downtown Montgomery lines of people, mostly black people, had begun to form at the bus stops, wearily waiting to go home after a long day's work.

Among those waiting was Mrs. Rosa Parks, a seamstress who made her living by altering women's dresses. All day long she stooped, with aching knees bent, with pins in her mouth, getting the hem line correct for women who wanted it just so, or other parts of their dresses changed to suit them.

Rosa Parks was tired, dead tired, from the day's work. Her feet hurt. She was hungry. She was in no mood to bear the command that came from the bus driver when she finally got on her bus. Neither she nor the bus driver knew it then, but his command to her and her refusal to obey helped to change America.

You see, in Montgomery, as in many other American cities and states then, there was a law that black people riding buses must take the rear seats and white people the front seats, even though all of them paid the same to ride. And if there was a shortage of seats, with more riders than seats available, then the black riders had to get up and stand while they rode so the white passengers could sit down.

So when the Montgomery bus on which Rosa Parks was riding that raw autumn evening became crowded, the bus driver ordered her to get up and go to the back of the bus so that a white man could sit down. She refused. This was breaking the law. The bus driver called the police; they arrested her and put her in jail.

She was an intelligent woman, long a good church member and active in many organizations in Montgomery to make the city better. She knew that the law was wrong concerning the seating arrangements on buses. Her black friends had long known it was wrong, and some had suffered for trying to change it.

We will not go into all the details here, for we do not have space, but Rosa Parks' refusal to obey anymore a wrong, un-Christian law changed America, and for the better.

Within a few hours the black citizens of Montgomery knew all about her being in jail. They formed a committee to deal with the situation. They elected a young man, a minister, whom the world had never heard of before, as chairman of the committee. His name was Reverend Dr. Martin Luther King, Jr., and he was pastor of the Dexter Avenue Baptist Church in Montgomery.

Under his leadership the black people of Montgomery decided that they would not ride the buses again until the laws on seating were changed. They would walk or form car pools. And they did. And the law was changed—not only in Montgomery, but in every other city and state that had such laws. And thereafter the name of Martin Luther King was known worldwide, for he and his committee changed things without violence.

Today, as citizens all over America ride buses, trains, and airplanes and sit wherever we choose, we might find such laws as Rosa Park faced hard to understand. We wonder what all the fuss was about.

But many other wrong practices continue, not only in America, but in other parts of the world as well. Some of them are considered right and legal, as millons of Americans did the bus seating arrangements before Rosa Parks' refusal to move on that eventful day in Mongomery long ago.

Because of these wrong practices and customs, many people suffer terribly. Changing them is not easy, but it is the Christian's duty to do so. One of the things we must change is our reliance on wars to settle disputes. With all the atomic weapons at hand, we cannot and must not have another war. It could destroy us all.

Can things be changed for the better? Some say they cannot be, that we must accept things as they are.

But Rosa Parks did not go along with this thinking. She changed America by her courage.

And God will give us all the strength to do what we should, as he gave it to her.

## 33 Why Does Vanilla Ice Cream Taste Good?

*Great is his steadfast love toward us. Ps. 117:2a*

Why does vanilla ice cream taste good? Or chocolate, or maple walnut, peppermint, peach, or any of the other flavors? Why do some things taste better than others? Why do potato chips taste better than grass or a hamburger better than alfalfa hay?

Why does fresh laundry dried out in the sun and wind have such a beautiful smell you like to bury your face in it and sniff? And why is a red, yellow, and gold sunset more beautiful than an average gray one? Why are not all sunsets gray and just alike? The sun would set just the same, you know.

Why are high mountains capped with snow so beautiful? Why are the roaring waves of the ocean surf so appealing to us all? Why cannot all the waves in the ocean be sort of low, flat, and even?

Stupid questions? Some might think so. That is, people who do not think or wonder very much.

Well, suppose all foods and drinks tasted just the same. And all smells were just one smell, all colors just one color, all sunsets gray, and no mountains? What a dull world it would be. We could probably exist, but how different life would be.

What I am talking about is the infinite variety God

has given to us in this great world of his. And not only in things and scenery, but in people. What a dull world if all people looked exactly the same, like they were squirted out of a machine, like macaroni or breakfast cereal. They would all have arms, legs, ears, and toes, but all would be look-alikes.

Most of us take this variety of God's world for granted. But there are people, for example, whose sense of taste has been destroyed by illness. Eating is just a chore for them. Others cannot smell. How sad, and dreary.

Somehow God has created us so that we can experience this truly beautiful universe of his with our bodies. The eye captures the colors of a rainbow or sunset and transmits the message to the brain that this view is not dull gray but a beautiful combination of blue, red, gold and yellow. The sight feeds our souls and inspires us.

To me it is all a miracle. So many miracles happen to us each day that we cannot list them all. As I write these words, great music is pouring out of my FM radio, sending me the compositions of Mozart. Why not just a lot of buzzing or a sound like a siren, instead of the beautifully played violins, piano, horns, and all the rest? Somehow the notes come out in such a fashion that they please my brain after striking my eardrums.

Perhaps you do not think all this is a miracle, but I do. And why do words of praise and love make us feel good in our hearts?

Because God, in his great power and wisdom, has created a world of variety, not only in his physical creations, but also in those things which thrill and inspire our minds and souls. Great poetry, great music, great lives—they lift us more than just reading a dictionary.

I cannot understand why all this is so. I can only accept it and say, "Thank you, God."

## 34 Is It Wrong to Waste?

*And they all ate and were satisfied. And they took up twelve baskets full of the broken pieces left over. Matt. 14:20*

Is it wrong to waste? If so, why? Why and how can we say that God wants us to use frugally and wisely the natural and human resources he has given us? Does it really hurt anybody if we are wasteful? After all, if we can afford it, why not? Is it not ours? we may ask.

More and more we are concluding that yes, it is wrong to waste. And if we do not stop wasting nature's gifts, there will not be any for the future. Until very recently we Americans thought our natural resources would never run out. Always there would be more oil, trees, rich soil, and minerals than we could ever use. How wrong we were. Now the world *conservation* is a big one for us. Save. Use wisely. Do not waste.

A few examples of waste: running the hot water in the shower a long time; not fixing a leaky faucet; a single drop per second from a hot water faucet leaks nine hundred gallons of hot water a year. Ask your parents how many dishes that would wash or baths it would provide and how much it would cost.

Other examples: making cars too big and powerful; not using car pools and buses when we could; leaving lights on in the house; throwing away instead of recycling bottles, cans, and papers; keeping buildings too warm in winter and too cool in summer. We could make a long list very quickly.

We Americans, with only one-twentieth of the world's population, use about one-half of its energy. We have gotten wasteful, and it is costing us a lot of money.

It took God millions of years to build up the top soil in America, but in only one hundred fifty years we have lost half of it through erosion due to wasteful farming methods. Every year we use up enough rich farmland for nonfarm purposes (such as roads, shopping plazas, homes) to make a strip of land half a mile wide from New York to San Francisco. Half the world's grapefruit is grown in Florida, but we are using the grapefruit lands so fast for other purposes that the price of grapefruit in our stores has increased.

As I write this, a great worldwide struggle between the nations is going on over the vast mineral riches lying on the oceans' floors. Should just the rich nations, like ours, with the right, expensive equipment, be allowed to dredge up these minerals as they please, or should they be allocated to all nations according to need?

We used to smile at the old saying Waste not, want not, but not anymore. We now know that waste is not only a sin, it is very expensive and can cause much suffering. Those who have much have no right to waste as long as there are so many of God's children without life's necessities. It is not right that so many of us are overfed while others starve.

When Jesus fed the multitude of five thousand, lots of food was left over. His disciples picked up twelve baskets full. Read about it in Matthew, chapter fourteen. We do not know what Jesus did with these twelve baskets full, but we do know that he did not waste them.

Waste is wrong. It is sinful. It is not necessary. And it can be stopped if we all pay attention to it.

## 35 You Do Not Have to Smoke

*You were called to freedom. Gal. 5:13a*

Have you ever been urged by some of your friends or by some older children to smoke? If you have not, you might be.

What you will say and do when that happens is really up to you. Nobody else can answer for you. It is your decision.

Sometimes boys and girls are offered cigarettes by their very best friends or by older brothers and sisters, who have already taken up the smoking habit.

Before you decide about smoking, you should really know what it does to you. First of all, smoking is not all that much fun, like eating ice cream or pizza. Nothing about our bodies craves tobacco naturally, like water and food. We do not get hungry for cigarettes before we take up the smoking habit. We can live without it.

What is wrong with smoking? Lots of things.

1. *It is expensive.* Most people who smoke spend more for the habit than they give to church and all charities. Just a pack of cigarettes a day costs around five dollars a week at the present rate.

2. *It is bad for your health.* Now maybe you do not care how strong your body is or how much endurance you have. If you do care, do not smoke. There are old people who have smoked for fifty years with no visible bad effects, but there are a lot with heart or lung trouble.

3. *It hurts other people.* Including people you love, especially those you love most. Those who live in the same apartment or house with smokers breathe in their stale smoke. Husbands and wives of some smokers have lung cancer.

4. *It is dangerous.* Many fires, including fatal ones, are caused by people going to sleep on a bed or couch with a lighted cigarette in their fingers. Innocent people are hurt and killed.

5. *It is not very smart.* In fact, not smart at all, though many steady smokers would not admit this. They know it is not smart but find it hard to quit. They wish they had never started.

If you can resist smoking these next few years, you can resist it the rest of your life. Each time you say no to smoking is a victory, not only for you, but for some other boy or girl you influence. And this is another big reason for not smoking—your influence on somebody who admires you. Just as misery loves company, so does courage love company.

No, you really do not have to smoke. Join the millions of other boys and girls who are saying no.

## 36 What Is Heaven Like?

---

*"No eye has seen, nor ear heard, nor the heart of man conceived, what God has prepared for those who love him." 1 Cor. 2:9b*

---

What is heaven like? Though all of us hope to go there when we die, we actually know almost nothing about what it will be like. When we take a journey here on earth, we usually know something about our destination. If our trip is a long and expensive one, ahead of time we get all kinds of printed matter telling us what to expect, what to see, and how much we will pay.

But about heaven, our most important destination of all, where we expect to spend all eternity, millions and millions of years, we know very little. Jesus, the one who knew and knows all about it, said very little about what it is actually like or where it is. Only in the fourteenth chapter of John did he say he was going to prepare a place for us. What a wonderful promise. Jesus, that great Friend, has prepared a place for you and me and all his other friends. And if he prepares a place, you can be sure it will be a wonderful one.

I have frequently wondered why Jesus did not describe heaven more. Of course, if he had, could we believe it? Are our minds that great? And it would take a lot of fun and surprise out of going to heaven—just as if parents told their children on December 20 exactly what to expect December 25. Maybe Jesus wants to surprise us.

What is heaven like? Will it be like here, only much better? with rivers, trees, animals, oceans, clouds, and all? Will it have vanilla ice cream? Or pizza with everything on it? Or will there be thick milk shakes or pink lemonade or World Series?

Will God provide beautiful sunsets and rainbows every day? Or soft summer rains, deep green restful forests, ocean beaches to play on, or deep grass to walk in barefooted?

Will there be music to hear and dance to? Or friends to play with and talk to? Will we need to eat, sleep, and rest? Will we ever have a toothache, get sick, or be unhappy?

For the answers to all these questions and lots more, we will just have to wait. We do get one clue about what heaven is like from the great disciple of Jesus, Paul. He said that we have never seen, heard of, or imagined anything like what God has prepared for those who love him. How wonderful.

Just think, no person has ever before or ever could imagine how great heaven is. If we thought for a hundred years, we would not be any closer to the answer.

Meanwhile, let us so live each day, being and doing what Christ wants us to be and do, that when we go to his heaven we will feel at home there. Best of all, he is not only with us here on earth but waits for us in heaven, which he has prepared for us. And because it is so wonderful, we need not fear but prepare to live there. It will be the most pleasant and joyous place to live any of us could imagine, and more.

## I Cannot Fix a Refrigerator Motor

37

*Now there are varieties of gifts, but the same Spirit. 1 Cor. 12:4*

I cannot repair a broken refrigerator motor. Can you? Neither can I repair an automobile carburetor or transmission, bake a cake, fly an airplane, remove an appendix, put a new roof on a house, nor run a computer. Nor can I do about 99 percent of the things that are done all around me every day, all of which are important to my welfare and comfort. When even a very simple thing goes wrong with my car, I have to take it to the filling station or garage for repairs.

How many things there are we cannot do in this complicated world. Yet, we survive, because there is always somebody around who can do them. Recently this thought came to me, How amazing it is that God put such a variety of abilities in us, so that no matter what needs to be done there is somebody trained and gifted in that particular job who can do it.

I am not completely without talents. I can type,

preach a sermon, raise tomatoes if the weather is right, drive a car, and put on wallpaper if the pattern is simple. But the fact is, I cannot deal with most of the complicated equipment we use today. Recently we had to call a repair man to fix our refrigerator door. It did not take him five minutes. Why could I have not done it? I did not know how, and if I had known, I did not have the right tools.

Once I knew a boy named Billy. With great difficulty Billy could read the school textbooks and pass his grades. But he could do anything with his hands. Give him a set of tools, and Billy could really use them. Today he is a successful housebuilder.

But as a boy I was all thumbs. I made good grades in school but was not good with tools nor was I a great athlete. I seldom hit a home run and was lucky to get a base hit now and then. When we chose up sides, I was seldom chosen among the first.

Now God has given us all some particular gift or talent; some people have many. We are lucky if we find out early in life how our talents match up with some specific kind of life work.

As for envying friends who seem more capable than we are, that is a waste of time and a form of self-pity. It is also a way of avoiding responsibility for our own lives. For we all have some abilities.

Yes, God has given us all something that is of value to the world, however small. In our complicated society there is some job, somewhere, that our talents will match up with. It may not be the most glamorous job, but it is an honest one, worth preparing for. And always and everywhere, there is a need for men and women who are Christians in their lives, who stand for the right, who try to help others. And we all have talents in that direction, no matter how unskilled we may be with our hands or thinking process.

Find out what you are best in and then develop those talents you like and succeed in most. God has work for you to do.

## 38 That Pesky Old Blue Daisy

*And that Christ may dwell in your hearts through faith; that you, being rooted and grounded in love, may . . . know the love of Christ which surpasses knowledge. Eph. 3:17-19a*

During the past thirty years our family has lived in three different towns and cities—all three homes with a nice green lawn. But with all three houses came a pesky weed that seems to follow us everywhere. It is what people call the blue daisy. Some call it the chicory plant. Its root, when dried, has been sometimes used, ground up and roasted, for an addition to coffee. I do not know what its scientific name is.

But this I do know. It is hard to get rid of, once established in one's yard. Mow it, cut it down, or whatever, and just a few days later you will see its pale blue flower here and there on the lawn.

And in the worst of the dry summer weather, when the grass looks dry and brown, the blue daisy prospers just the same. While you do not mow the lawn because it is too dry for the grass to grow, the blue daisy shoots higher and higher, up to three and four feet.

Try to pull it up? No way. You cannot. For its root has grown way down deep into the soil, seeking moisture and nourishment. This kind of deep root is called a taproot. Many plants and some trees, such as the longleaf yellow pine tree of our Southlands, have a taproot. Storms may break the trees down but never uproot them, so deep is their taproot in the earth.

But the world's largest living thing, the giant sequoia, or redwood tree of California, does not have a taproot; it spreads its roots widely, not deeply, intertwining them with the roots of other redwood trees. When a hard storm comes these giant trees may blow over, taking other trees with them. No taproot.

Another taproot plant is the tea weed of the South. During the Civil War its leaves were dried and used for tea. From years' experience as a gardener in the South, I can tell you that the tea weed is very tough, hard to pull up. It has a taproot.

These plants with a taproot, whether weeds or trees, have a lesson for us. It is their taproot that makes them strong.

Certainly a strong body, founded on hard exercise and training, provides us with stamina to overcome fatigue and disease. Good study habits provide us with a trained mind that can solve problems. Practice at a skill until it is mastered—whether in sports, music, athletics, or school studies—creates in us an attitude of always doing our best and completing a task once begun.

We need to pray, meditate, study the Bible, and think about God very much if we are to have a spiritual taproot that will give us strength in times of need and adversity. This is done little by little, day by day, just as the blue daisy sinks its roots just a fraction of an inch deeper each day. And as the blue daisy draws its strength from deep in the earth, so we draw ours from God.

## 39 Only an Orange for Christmas?

*"A man's life does not consist in the abundance of his possessions."* Luke 12:15b

Suppose you woke up bright and early next Christmas morning after all those days of waiting and hoping that Santa Claus got your letter, went into the room where your family holds its Christmas, looked at your stocking, and there it would be—limp and empty—and no package under the Christmas tree. No, not quite empty would the stocking be. Down in the toe is something round. Pull it out. An orange (an actual orange in a sock or stocking can illustrate).

Just a plain orange. The kind you can see in any supermarket or corner grocery any day of the week.

Only an orange for Christmas? Suppose that

actually happened to you. Would you feel like someone was playing tricks on you? Possibly so.

Well, it did happen to somebody I loved very much. My mother, whom I loved very dearly. She died several years ago at the age of ninety.

She once told me that when she was a little girl most people where she lived had very little cash money. The big stores like we have now did not exist, and if they had, people did not have money to buy the items in them. So, one Christmas, all she got was an orange.

Was she unhappy? Not at all. She said she was thrilled as much by that orange as her own children were later with far more expensive and numerous Christmas gifts. She told me that she kept that orange serveral days, feeling its smooth skin, smelling its nice aroma, admiring its color, taking it to bed with her, and finally eating it slowly, to make its taste last.

Only an orange for Christmas? No, she had some far more valuable gifts—a good home with two parents who loved her, good health, and so many other blessings.

Jesus tried to tell us that it is not the things we own that can provide us happiness. They can only provide comfort. Once I saw an eight-year-old girl actually get bored while opening the huge pile of Christmas gifts under the tree. My mother was happier with just one orange.

Some of us have so many possessions we get bored with them. The things that make us happy cannot be bought—love, friendship, the warmth of friends and family, the knowledge that we are loved and that we love others. And most precious of all is

God's love revealed to us through his precious Son Jesus Christ.

Only an orange for Christmas? Most of us have far more precious gifts all year long. Perhaps if we only got an orange in our stocking next Christmas, we would think just how blessed we truly are.

## 40  Words Can Hurt

*The tongue is a fire. James 3:6a*

There is an old saying that may not always be true.

> Sticks and stones may break my bones,
> But words will never hurt me.

Words can hurt. They can hurt a lot, not just one person or a few, but many, perhaps a whole nation. Who of us has not been hurt deeply, perhaps with the pain lasting for days or weeks, by the careless or intentionally cruel words said to us or about us? How I remember some of the unkind words said to me, and how much I regret those I have spoken about others or to others.

The third chapter of the letter by James, Jesus' disciple, in the New Testament, is all about what a terrible thing the tongue is when not controlled by its owner. Read it for yourself, for it says so clearly how dangerous is a careless or malicious tongue.

When I was a boy I often had to wear my older brother's last year's clothing that he had outgrown. It did not always fit, despite my mother's alterations. The sleeves could only be lengthened just so much, and my long arms stuck way out of them. My friends recognized the suit for what it was, my brother's last year's clothes. After these fifty years I can still remember a little girl's mean remark about how the suit was too short for me. I can laugh about it now, but I could not then.

Along the way I too have probably said many things that hurt other people. Sometimes I may have meant them; other times I was merely careless or lacked imagination about how my words might affect those hearing them.

Words have no weight, taste, smell, or feel. They disappear forever into thin air once uttered unless recorded, which few are. But how long lasting they can be in their effect upon the listener. Sometimes we can remember for years the very sound and tone of unkind words spoken to us.

Furthermore, though their sound disappears instantly when spoken, they can be kept intact in memory or in writing for years or for centuries. Jesus wrote none of his great sayings. His disciples remembered them and wrote them down years later.

Words can cause pain, but they can also give pleasure. Words of praise, affection, approval, and admiration, coming from the right person, somebody we love or admire, can ring warmly in our hearts for a long time, often making a whole day or week a good one for us.

How can we avoid saying mean things? First, put yourself in the other person's shoes and try to think how you would feel. Next, always try to think twice before you speak. Not always easy, but try it. Next, say nothing bad about anybody. Even if a bad rumor is true, it might be best not to repeat it. Next, always try to say something positive about people. Jesus praised his disciples, calling them his friends, a great compliment. Finally, read for yourself the third chapter of the Letter of James in the Bible.

## 41 Willie Stargell's Strike-out Record

---

*We are hard-pressed on all sides, but we are never frustrated; we are puzzled, but never in despair. We are persecuted, but are never deserted: we may be knocked down but we are never knocked out! 2 Cor. 4:8-9, Phillips*

---

What major league baseball player has struck out more than any other player who ever lived? Wilver Dornell Stargell, better known as Willie Stargell. No other player—not even the mighty Babe Ruth, Micky Mantle, Willie Mayes, or Hank Aaron—comes even close to Willie Stargell's strike-out record.

Willie Stargell is the player, more than any other, who in 1979, put the Pittsburgh Pirates in the World Series against the favored Baltimore Orioles for the world championship. Small wonder he was voted the most valuable player in that series, won by

Pittsburgh. By his enthusiasm, courage, brilliant fielding, and hitting just at the right times, he literally pulled the Pirates from underdogs to world champions.

Yes, he can hit when it counts, when men are on base or the bases are loaded. He can knock out hits, two baggers, three baggers, or home runs when it matters. But he has also struck out more than any other man in National or American League history.

With that kind of strike-out record, you might think Willie Stargell would get discouraged and quit. And maybe he felt like quitting more than once. For example, the Pirates are behind, the bases are loaded, and Willie gets up to bat. Yes, as we said, Willie can hit when it counts; but remember that he is also the all-time strike-out champion, having missed the ball with his bat more times than any other player.

How does he feel when he strikes out with bases loaded? Not good, we can assure you. But he has kept on practicing and swinging, never giving up, earning the respect of millions.

Did you ever strike out, not in baseball, but in something very important to you? Have you failed where all could see? Have you honestly tried but were defeated? Have you even gotten to the point where you felt there was no use going on, trying again, putting forth more effort? Well, Willie Stargell probably felt that way also more than once.

If Stargell teaches us anything, it is to keep on trying if we feel that what we are doing is the right thing, keep doing our best and trying all the time to improve ourselves by constant study and practice, seeking new ways of achievement.

Jesus, great as he was, had many moments of trial and disappointment. He, too, got discouraged. No doubt the lowest point in his life was on the cross when he cried out, "My God, my God, why did you forsake me?" If Jesus felt like that, then he certainly knows how we feel in our times of failure and disappointment.

Yes, all through life, not just when we are young, we will probably have times of failure. That is life. Sometimes it is our fault; sometimes it is not. But regardless, it might pay us to remember the example of baseball's strike-out king Willie Stargell, the Pittsburgh Pirate hero.

## 42 She Has Knitted a Few Thousand Mittens

*"She has done what she could." Mark 14:8a*

In the Emmanuel Congregational United Church of Christ Church in Watertown, New York, the Sunday school has a beautiful tradition. Each Christmas, in addition to the huge Christmas tree erected in the church, a smaller tree is put up —spruce, fir, or balsam, usually about eight or ten feet high.

No decorations, not even a star at the top, are put on this tree. Then, two Sundays before Christmas Day the children celebrate mitten-tree Sunday. They bring in gifts of warm mittens, gloves, scarves, and knitted caps and decorate the tree with them.

Within five minutes after they start, the tree is a riot of color, limbs bent low with the weight of these warm things for distant children's heads, hands, and necks. All colors of the rainbow and then some, with most of the items hand knitted. After Christmas these items are shipped to Church World Service, the Protestant relief agency, and it distributes them to children, overseas and in this country, who need them badly.

The mitten-tree tradition in Emmanuel Church goes back over twenty-five years, and we hope it does not stop as long as there are children somewhere with cold fingers and no mittens. The mitten-tree story in itself is thrilling, but at Emmanuel Church there is a new aspect of it we would like to share.

When the mitten tree was first started there, the minister told a story about a little girl at a scene where mittens were to be distributed. Just as she got to the head of the line and reached out for her mittens, the supply ran out. There were no more and no place where she could get any. This story so touched one lady member of the church she could not get it out of her mind. It haunted her—this story that may have come true more than once.

So, to make sure that there would be fewer little girls or boys without warm things to wear she began to collect scraps and bits of yarn—any size, color, make, or composition. All year long she knitted, using these bits and pieces. And interestingly enough the mittens, scarfs, and woolen hats she knits look more beautiful because various colors are blended together instead of just one color.

She has done this year after year. Early in

December each year, she takes the year's accumulation of her work, usually about one hundred complete sets of caps and mittens, to the minister in secret. She wants nobody to know about her work.

The story about this anonymous lady knitter has spread, and people for many miles around bring and mail scraps of yarn to the church where she secretly picks them up. At home she may sit for hours knitting while watching television or talking with her family, so automatic are her fingers' movements as they click, click, click the knitting needles. She must have made at least two thousand sets of mittens and hats in the past twenty years. No, not enough to warm all the shivering little tots in the world, but enough to make two thousand of them more comfortable.

I believe this is the kind of true story that makes Jesus happy, don't you?

## 43 Are There Animals in Heaven?

---

*"And the beasts of the field shall be at peace with you."* Job 5:23b

---

Will animals be in heaven? Do animals have souls? I have been a minister many, many years, and children have asked me these two questions as often as any other.

If you ever had a favorite pet—a dog, cat, horse, pony, canary, parrakeet—and it died, you remember how it almost broke your heart, and you wanted there to be a heaven for animals. All of us who have had faithful pets have hoped that God would have a heaven for them.

My wife and our children have had dogs who seemed so much a part of the family that we cried when they died. They seemed to love us so much, were so faithful and friendly, so eager to please, seemed so grateful for our praise, favors, and friendship that they seemed almost human. They were happy when we were happy, and when we were sad they seemed to sense it and became sad with us.

Horses, too, become so close to their owners that they also seem to know their feelings. It may seem uncanny how animals seem to read our minds. So many true stories have been told about animals' returning affection to human beings. And every few months we read in the newspapers about a lost dog or cat who returned to their owners by themselves scores or hundreds of miles away. Why and how do they do it? Only great affection would account for it.

Because they live in the deep ocean, dolphins are not our pets like dogs and cats, but from what we know of them they are also friendly, warmhearted animals. Many true stories, beginning in ancient times, tell how dolphins have rescued drowning seamen.

The Bible says nothing about animals having souls or going to heaven. But people keep asking, "Why not?" Will we not have there the same devoted pets who have given us more comfort and understanding than other people sometimes? I do not know and would not say either way. That is for God to decide.

But we do know that animals are God's creatures and are therefore to be treated with kindness. Something in us all rebels at outright cruelty to animals, and most states now have laws against such cruelty. Just a few years ago, animals' owners could do with them whatever they liked—starve, beat, or whatever. I am glad that the public now forbids such treatment.

We know that many animals have human feelings toward each other. A mother bear, bird, or tiger will give her life for her offspring, and most animals do as much, in their own way, to bring up their young as human beings. We may call them just animals, but none of the higher animals abuse their children as some human parents do.

If animals have no souls and this life is all there is for them, then we have an extra obligation, do we not, to make this life of theirs a good one?

We know that animals have feelings of fear, pain, hunger, thirst, affection just like we do. They like praise and shrink from criticism. They fear a harsh tone of voice and respond to love.

Do animals have souls? Do they go to heaven? I do not know. That is for God to decide. But they are God's creatures. The Indians call them brothers. So, let us be kind to them.

# Life's Sacrifice Plays

---

*"He who finds his life will lose it, and he who loses his life for my sake will find it." Matt. 10:39*

---

In baseball what is a sacrifice play? It is a hit that will almost certainly put the batter out but that advances another player on his team to another base. Sometimes the hit takes the form of a fly but more frequently a bunt.

You must have seen a sacrifice play more than once if you watch baseball. The manager of the team at bat has a player on first or second or perhaps two players on separate bases. He wants to advance them toward scoring position, that is, closer to home plate. So he directs the batter to make a sacrifice play.

Usually in bunting, the batter holds the bat quite differently from usual and sort of pushes the ball instead of swinging at it. The best bunts are those too far for the catcher to retrieve, preferably toward third base, very close to the foul line, and fast enough to be out of easy reach for the pitcher. This does not keep the batter from being put out at first, which he had planned, but it does prevent the opposing team from getting their hands on the ball quickly enough to put out the batter's teammate(s). A bunt usually rolls along the ground, thus slowing it down.

So, if the bunt is successful the batter is put out at first, but his team is in a better scoring position. In other words, the batter has sacrificed his chances of getting a hit, getting on base, and, of course, any chance of scoring. Hence, it is called a sacrifice play.

Too many sacrifice plays in one season can severely lower a player's season hitting average, a very precious thing to most baseball players. So, the more a player helps his team with sacrifice plays, the more he hurts his own record. *Sacrifice* is the correct word for it. And often the best hitters are called on for sacrifice plays.

Making sacrifice plays does not occur just on the baseball field. Have you ever done things that helped others—not just individuals, but groups, such as teams, Scout troups, and your church—that got you little praise or credit? Surely most of us have.

Parents make sacrifice plays all the time—giving up, for us, things they would like and never complaining—without their children even knowing of their sacrifices.

Many great scientists, statesmen, and other public leaders sacrifice themselves in hard work, long hours, study, and service, so that others may be helped. Humanity has advanced this way.

In nature, mother birds will give up their lives to protect their little ones. So will many other animals. Sacrifice plays.

Growing up involves our willingness to do things that give us little credit so that what we believe in may succeed. The great example of this is the willingness of Jesus Christ to be crucified rather than give up the way of love and forgiveness. He made the greatest of all sacrifice plays.

When you see a sacrifice bunt the next time,

remember that it not only takes skill, but that the batter puts his team ahead of his own batting average.

## Learn Something Now for New Year's Season  45

---

*Fear not, for I am with you, be not dismayed, for I am your God; I will strengthen you, I will help you. Isa. 41:10a*

---

In addition to the New Year's resolutions that I hope you are making, I would like to make a further suggestion that can make the coming twelve months bring some good tidings to you: Learn to do at least one new thing before next January 1.

Set your mind to learn some new skill, accomplishment, body of knowledge, hobby, or whatever, however small it may be. Is there something that you have really wanted to accomplish, that you are capable of doing, that is within your financial reach, that would bring you or others happiness, but you just have not gotten around to? Then why not make these coming twelve months the time to do it?

Lots of people pooh-pooh New Year's resolutions. True, some such resolutions are quickly forgotten, but they do not have to be. It is always easy to say, "I won't even try." And you are never too old.

When I became fifty-one, perhaps an old age to

you, I made a resolution to learn to ride a bicycle. I had never ridden a bike. When I was a boy in rural Mississippi, we had horses to ride but no bikes. So, I never learned. But how I wanted to.

So, I got out my son's bike, practiced on it for many days in the backyard, then practiced at a nearby shopping plaza Sunday afternoons when there were few cars around, and pretty soon I was pedaling down the city streets with the best of them. How glad I was that I followed through on that New Year's resolution.

When we were sixty-three years old, my wife and I had never bowled. So, we resolved to learn. We have had ever so much fun since. We overcame our fear of failure and found that many others were no better bowlers than we had become.

A main reason many of us do not attempt new skills is fear—fear of failure and fear of others' laughing at us. When I first began bike riding, the kids in the neighborhood had a lot of fun at my expense. But I kept on, and soon they were trying to help me. We became friends because I needed them.

Surely God wants us to develop our talents to the fullest. We can believe that Jesus did. He was probably the best carpenter in Nazareth, or any-where. The more competent, or skilled, we are, the greater service we can be to others and to God.

In closing, let me admit that I am still afraid to try something I want ever so much to do and never did because there were no sidewalks or paved streets in my boyhood home. I cannot roller-skate. And I am afraid to try for at my age I might fall and break a bone. I simply must watch others roller-skate and long to do the same. Perhaps in heaven there are roller-skating rinks, where I can learn without worrying about broken bones.

## *Where Does Music Come From?*  46

---

*Praise him with trumpet sound;*
*praise him with lute and harp!*
*Praise him with timbrel and dance;*
*praise him with strings and pipe!*
*Praise him with sounding cymbals;*
*praise him with loud clashing cymbals!*
*Ps. 150:3-5*

---

You can not see it, touch it, feel or smell it. It weighs nothing, not even so much as a postage stamp. And it disappears the split second it comes to us, leaving no trace of ever being here. Yet, while present it provides us much pleasure, joy, and inspiration, recalls old memories of times long ago, stirs up all kinds of wonderful feelings inside, and can make us happy or sad.

We can hear it. We are talking about music. Music comes, strikes our eardrums, and then proceeds quickly on to the next note, leaving a trail of emotions, invisible but very real.

Where does music come from? I do not mean the piece of paper that gives a musician directions for playing, nor the records and tapes that reproduce the sounds imagined by some composer, maybe two hundred years ago, perhaps only last year. We buy sheet music, records, and tapes from the music store.

But where did the original composer get these notes? How could he or she used the seven keys from C to B, with all their sharps and flats and other variations, and so arrange them on a sheet of paper that decades or even centuries later musicians, either alone or in bands and symphony orchestras, could play these exact notes as the composer recorded them on paper? From where did the tunes come?

Originally these tunes did not exist in actual sound but as invisible, mental assemblages of sounds nobody ever heard or imagined before. For instance, most of the tunes in your own church's hymnbook did not exist two centuries ago. Now they are so well known that many people in your church could play, hum, or whistle them from memory. They now exist in people's minds, these tunes that did not exist at all not so long ago.

We do know that most great music comes to trained musicians like Beethoven, Mozart, and Bach, whose minds are already directed toward the reception of music and trained to put it down in notes when it comes. But some writers of very popular music cannot read or play music, only pick it out with one finger on the piano. This is true of Irving Berlin, who has written the words and music of so many of America's best-loved songs.

We do know that many great tunes come quickly and suddenly without warning to composers. Do these composers make up the music or merely do what the term *compose* means, "to put together"? Maybe a mixture of both. The great composer

Mozart said that his music came to him suddenly and in large quantities and that as quickly as he could he recorded it in notes on paper.

Could we not say that, like so many other of God's blessings, music comes from him and that there is simply no other explanation? Like his other gifts, music can be turned into a bad thing, but seldom is.

The great composer Handel said that as he silently heard the great themes of the *Messiah*, which we play at Christmas and Easter, that heaven itself seemed to open up to him as the great themes of that masterpiece came flooding into his trained mind, completely filling it with the great sounds that inspire us today.

Perhaps the real source of music will always remain a mystery to humanity—something to receive and enjoy more than something we invent.

Very few of us will ever be known as composers, but we are all putting our lives together. And from God come all kinds of great thoughts and feelings. They come from the Bible, from other people, from our own willingness to receive God's truth. They find expression, not from notes set down on paper, but in the lives we lead.

*Serendipity*  47

---

*"Seek first his kingdom and his righteousness, and all these things shall be yours as well."* Matt. 6:33

---

What is serendipity? It is not a new ice cream treat or a disease or a chemical. Serendipity is seeking one thing you want and in the process finding something else of great value.

The word *serendipity* comes from an old fable about the Three Princes of Serendip. Serendip was the ancient name for the large island we now call Sri Lanka, just southeast off the tip of India. According to this story the three princes, all sons of a wise king, were sent by their father on a wandering journey to find a certain person. He did this to test them and see which one was most suited to succeed him on the throne. In their journeys the three sons never did find the man they sought, but they found other things very wonderful in the process.

No doubt you have already experienced serendipity in your own life and did not know it. We all have. But let us examine a few examples.

Christopher Columbus set out to find India by sailing westward from Spain in 1492 over the Atlantic Ocean. People called him crazy. True, he never reached India, though he thought he had at first and even named the people there Indians. He did not reach India, but he discovered America.

The Scottish scientist Sir Alexander Fleming was looking for something else when he discovered that a bacterium called penicillin could destroy all sorts of disease germs. From his serendipitous discovery come all kinds of useful antibiotic drugs.

Pearl divers in Asia not only bring up these fine, lustrous jewels, but also can use all the oysters, whether or not they contain pearls, for selling and eating.

A boy or girl who exercises every day to get on an

athletic team may not make the team but has a stronger, more vigorous body as a result. Serendipity.

Young people who form regular study habits and learn to complete school projects on time are learning habits that later will make them successful in jobs. Serendipity.

When we are friendly and go out of our way to be sympathetic and helpful to those in need, we not only become finer persons inside but also make lots of friends. Serendipity.

Serendipity works in reverse also. If we develop evil, hostile, destructive, lazy, mean, unfriendly habits in life, then these ways will be reflected back on us. Jesus told us, "Whatever you wish that men would do to you, do so to them." We call this the Golden Rule.

Though he did not use the word *serendipity*, Jesus described it when he said, "Seek first his kingdom and his righteousness, and all these things will be yours as well." Seek first God's will, and you will be blessed in ways you cannot dream of. Serendipity.

## *Your Body Does Not Belong to You* 48

*I appeal to you therefore, brethren, by the mercies of God, to present your bodies as a living sacrifice, holy and acceptable to God, which is your spiritual worship. Rom. 12:1*

Your body does not belong to you, no matter how many times you might say, "my body." It never did belong to you and never will. You did not make it, did you?

You live in it; you hurt when it hurts; you feel good when it feels good.

You feed it, clothe it, wash it, comb its hair, brush its teeth, exercise it, pour all sorts of crazy foods and drinks inside, and once a day lay it down for about eight hours of rest and sleep that it should have. For about one-third of its existence, the body you call yours is asleep.

Of course we speak of my body and our body quite naturally, but factually it is not correct—they are God's bodies. They all belong to him. This body I call mine, I occupy as long as I live, and then it is returned to the earth from which it was made.

God made our bodies. No human scientist will ever be wise enough or know enough to explain the many thousands of complicated things going on at any given moment in any human body. There are over ten thousand enzymes alone in every one of the billions of cells in our body not to mention all the genes that determine our physical characteristics.

We never appreciate fully how wonderful our body is until it gets sick or hurts. Just a small part, like an aching tooth, makes us realize suddenly how great is perfect health.

And because the body we live in belongs to God, we need to take the best possibe care of it, so it can do his work better. Personally, I always took better care of something I had borrowed than if it belonged to me, such as a car or typewriter or an article of clothing. So, as this body I live in is God's, I should treat it with extra care. And not just our bodies—but our minds, talents, personalities, and all that we have and are, including our money, our jobs, and the families we call our own. They, too, belong to God. The Bible says it so well: "The earth is the Lord's and the fulness thereof."

What a serious thing it is for nations to think that the land and waters within their borders are theirs to treat as they wish and extract all the profit they can in this generation, right now. This attitude is causing our polluted rivers and lakes, our poisoned lands, our scrubby forests, our trash-littered city streets.

Fortunately we are recognizing our mistake about mistreating our environment. We are cleaning up God's land, rivers, lakes, ocean, sky, and city streets. This is called conservation. Those who lead in it should be among our national heroes.

Our own personal environment, the closest to us, is our body. When it suffers through neglect or abuse or by wrong substances, such as drugs, alcohol, and improper foods, being put into it, we suffer. Lack of exercise makes it flabby and of less value to us.

Those of us blessed with bodies and minds that work well should be extra careful not to eat or drink substances we know are harmful. Be good to God's body that you are occupying, and it will be good to you.

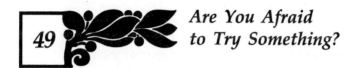

# 49 Are You Afraid to Try Something?

---

*"I came that they may have life, and have it abundantly."* John 10:10b

---

Are you afraid to try something you would like to do very much? If you are, let me tell you a secret—many other people are, too.

Yes, if you could see inside people's minds, as if there were a magic window over them, you would see all sorts of fears, hesitations, timidity, and awkwardness inside. You are not alone in your fears. Many people are like you, including those who often seem so brave and bold on the outside.

One thing that gave me great difficulty as a small boy in school was making the figure 2 on the blackboard. For some reason my hand just would not perform correctly when I got up to do my work for the teacher. She was very kind about it, but the other children, sensing my fear and awkwardness, made me all the more nervous with their giggles. How embarrassed and ashamed I was. Finally, my mother heard about it and taught me at home to make a 2. How proud I was the first time I walked up to the blackboard and wrote it without hesitation in bold, thick chalk. The giggles ceased. My fears ceased.

Also, for some reason I could never make a proper bow knot with my shoelaces. Somehow in my failure, I invented another kind of bowknot, my own, which I still use today.

One way boys and girls can learn something new that they want so badly to learn is to want it so bad it hurts. This is called motivation. In professional baseball it is called desire when a player tries so hard he stretches himself all the way, like jumping that extra inch to catch a fly.

A good way to learn a skill is to practice in secret. I once knew a man who did not learn to dance until he was twenty years old. He was afraid of being laughed at if he tried in public. So he practiced alone, using a home record player. He conquered his fears through practice.

One of America's favorite stories is how the timid John Alden, way back in Plymouth days in Massachusetts, was afraid to ask Priscilla Mullins to marry him. The brave soldier Miles Standish was courting Priscilla, but she did not love him. She kept waiting for John to propose to her. Finally she spoke those famous words, "Why don't you speak for yourself, John?" It shows that some of our great national leaders were hesitant and shy, too.

God has given abilities and talents to us all. True, some have more than others. Some people seem to learn things so easily. They acquire friends, skills, good grades, athletic achievements seemingly without effort.

Most of us are not like that. We have to try harder. But that is no excuse for not trying. And what a wonderful feeling when we try and try and do something well enough to be proud, or at least not ashamed.

Pray to God to give you strength and courage. Then do your best. Work hard, practice, and pray. A lot of your fears will vanish.

# The Timid Turtle Sticks His Neck Out

**50**

---

*"Fear not, nor be afraid." Isa. 44:8a*

---

What a strange creature is the turtle, wearing its skeleton on the outside of its body. Turtles of different species go by the names of turtle, terrapin, and tortoise. They range in size from a tiny terrapin a small child can lift with one hand to the giant sea trutle, weighing over a thousand pounds.

And they are among the earth's oldest living creatures. The same kind of turtle we see today was around 100 million years ago, swimming around dodging the dinosaurs. They have managed to survive many species of larger, more aggressive animals.

Besides being very durable, turtles have one very unusual quality because of their shells. In order to move forward or swim, they have to stick their necks outside their shell, look around, and then get going, whether on land or in water. No forward movement without the neck stuck out. Otherwise, the turtle stays right there in the same spot.

I have often thought how much like turtles we are. We have to stick out our necks to advance, to grow up, to become the kind of persons God wants us to be.

Like the turtle many of us have a shell, sometimes of our own making. Not the horny tough shell they have, but we can develop other kinds of mental and spiritual shells that can handicap our forward movement just the same. Some of these invisible shells are:

*The shell of shyness.* Some of us are too shy to speak to others in a friendly way, too shy to smile at people, even when we would like to ever so much, too shy to shake hands. Or look somebody in the eye or talk in a natural way and share our feelings with them. We can be too shy to call people up on the telephone for a friendly conversation or ask them to go somewhere we would both like to go.

To ourselves our shy feeling is shyness, but to others it may come across as unfriendliness. Others may think we do not like them when all the time it is shyness. The answer, sticking out our head like the turtle, so to speak, is to make ourselves act friendly, not just feel friendly inside. If this is done, the shell of shyness gradually disappears, and we are free from a terrible burden.

*The shell of selfishness.* This shell causes us to do things with this thought in mind, *What's in it for me?* Not what can I do for others, but what can they do for me? Really, it is a disease called me-itis.

Me-itis does not fool others for long. They soon catch on to our motive of selfishness and gradually leave us alone, withdrawing from us. The cure for me-itis is to think, *what can I do for others* instead of, *what can they do for me*. The shell of selfishness grows heavier with each passing year, so get rid of it as soon as you can. It is an ugly, ever-growing shell if not gotten rid of.

*The shell of self-pity.* Otherwise called the shell of feeling sorry for ourself. This shell not only isolates us from others but also makes them grow tired of hearing our complaints about how mistreated we are. Some people do not care after they have heard our troubles a time or two.

Did you ever hear of Fanny Crosby? Perhaps not, but you have probably sung some of the songs she wrote. Fanny Crosby was born blind in 1820 and lived to be ninety-eight. Many people think she was America's greatest hymn writer. She wrote over six thousand hymns, many of which are still sung in churches a hundred years after they were written.

Though blind all her life, Fanny Crosby was not bitter or resentful because of her misfortune, and her hymns show the great joy and peace that comes from Christ. Here is a poem that she wrote at the age of eight and that we should all read when we feel sorry for ourselves and retreat into the shell of self-pity.

### Content

Oh, what a happy child I am,
Although I cannot see!
I am resolved that in this world
Contented I would be.

How many blessings I enjoy
That other people don't!
So weep or sigh because I'm blind,
I cannot, nor I won't!

So many people, like Fanny Crosby, have troubles worse than ours, but if we are foolish we can keep our heads inside the shell of self-pity, feeling sorrier and sorrier for ourself and boring other people with our troubles.

A good cure for the shell of self-pity is to seek out

those who have troubles greater than ours and reach out to them in some friendly way. The more we do this, the lighter our shell of self-pity becomes, and pretty soon it disappears. How much better we feel then.

Do you have some kind of shell you want to get rid of? Then stick out your neck like the turtle, and if you do it often enough the shell will go away.

## *Learn to Tread Water*  51

---

*They who wait for the Lord shall renew their strength. Isa. 40:31a*

---

Do you know how to tread water? If you can, you might save your life with this skill someday.

The word *tread* means literally to "walk." We all know that the only person who ever walked on water the same as on land was Jesus, when he walked to his disciples on the Sea of Galilee. But by treading we mean making motions in the water similar to walking. Instead of moving forward, as in swimming, one stays in one place with one's head above the surface. Not going anywhere, but not going under either. That is the purpose of treading water—to stay afloat with the least expenditure of energy, either to just rest or to stay afloat in a situation of danger until help can come.

The motions of treading water are simple—just pushing the feet down as in riding a bicycle and waving the arms up and down, more or less extended to the sides, with hands cupped to get the greatest resistance to the water. And it is best to have the least possible part of one's head above the surface. Just having the nose in the air is the main thing. We strongly recommend that everyone learn to tread water. It is really very simple to master.

Do we not all feel sometimes as if we are not getting anywhere or doing the things we think we should? Sure we do. Some things do not seem to work right for us. But that feeling comes to us all. Then is the time to just keep plodding, even if we seem to stay in one place.

A well-known piano teacher told me once that she advises her pupils to practice daily, especially at those times when they do not seem to be advancing. If they practice as they should daily, she said, soon they will move forward. In a way she is telling them to tread water and not give up.

Adults get this feeling just like children. In fact, they get it worse. And not for just a few days or weeks but sometimes for years at a time. But they cannot quit in despair; they have to go on.

It was true back in Bible days. That is why the Bible is so great—it describes the experiences of people back then just as we have them today. The same human emotions. They have not changed any since the time of David, Moses, Elijah, and Jesus.

The writers of Psalms and Isaiah tell us several times to "wait for the Lord," and he will give us strength and help us. Back then many of God's children must have felt very blue and downcast and needed encouragement. The prophets told them to wait for the Lord—not to give up.

Treading water. Please learn, for it may save your life. And not just from drowning. Keeping on going helps us in many other ways.

## Giving Up Good Things for a Better Thing

52

---

*"The kingdom of heaven is like a merchant in seach of fine pearls, who, on finding one pearl of great value, went and sold all that he had and bought it." Matt. 13:45-46*

---

In Jesus' time, as in ours, pearls were considered of great value. Jesus lived in a part of the world that produced then, as well as now, some of the finest pearls in the world.

Perfectly round, large pearls were expensive then and are now. A string of large, perfectly matched pearls costs many hundreds of dollars.

In the parable of the pearl dealer, related by Jesus, there was a merchant who went in search of fine pearls. He found one, the largest and most beautiful he had ever seen. So badly did he want it that he went and sold everything he owned and bought that pearl—the perfect one. His house, lands, clothing, jewelry, livestock, everything went. So badly did he want that pearl. He had to give up a lot of good things to get the best, but he did give them up. His dream was now fulfilled.

In a way we are like that pearl dealer. In our dreams we wish to be somebody good, great, and admired. And how do we go about becoming so? In the same way the pearl merchant of Jesus' day did, by being willing to sacrifice the lesser things for the greater.

For instance, in mastering our school subjects we have to choose them over what might be some very pleasant alternatives. We cannot have both. The same applies to attaining athletic skills, hobbies, musical talent, and artistic abilities. We give up time spent on other things to achieve them.

Would you like to know a lot about the Bible? Then I suggest you start with the Gospel of Matthew and read the New Testament right through several times. Then read the Old Testament the same way. Soon you will have a real pearl—a knowledge of the Bible. Memorize the great passages; they will stay with you through life. Attend church every Sunday morning. Even Jesus had to choose that he would attend church, which he did regularly, over other ways of spending that time required.

All of us face the choice of choosing that greatest pearl of any price—becoming a disciple and follower of Jesus in preference to living our lives selfishly. No other decision is as important as the one in which you give your life to Christ. Now, while you are young, is the time to do it.

There may be hardships and sacrifices because we take this step, make this decision, and pattern our lives after his. But if we are faithful to him, he will give us that pearl of great price—being called his friend.